'9.95

More
More
Quality
Quality
Circle Time
Circle Time

JENNY MOSLEY

The Whole School Quality Circle Time
Model can help improve and maintain
high standards of behaviour and
discipline."

Guidance Notes from DfEE on
Good Practice – Key Principles

More Quality Circle Time
LL01106
ISBN 1 85503 270 8
© Jenny Mosley
© illustrations Sami Sweeten
All rights reserved
First published 1998
Reprinted 2000, 2001

LDA, Duke Street, Wisbech, Cambs, PE13 2AE, UK.
3195 Wilson Drive, Grand Rapids, MI 49544, USA.

Contents

SECTION 3

SECTION 4

MENTAL HEALTH WARNING

SOME CLASSES ARE NOT READY FOR CIRCLE TIME

What do I mean by this warning?

I know of teachers who, fired up either by attending a Circle Time course or reading a book, have gone back to their classrooms convinced that Circle Time will provide the 'quick fix' they've long been waiting for. This response is a recipe for disaster!

Picture the scenario. A stressed teacher is trying to organise the children into a circle. Some children kick over, or 'accidentally' fall off, their chairs. Whole groups of friends adamantly refuse to be separated, and nobody will sit next to Wayne. The children seem totally incapable of remembering the ground rules and prefer to throw rather than pass the 'talking object'. Exit one disillusioned teacher.

Low-level disruption, tiredness, stress and a lack of effective and consistent behaviour policies mean that many teachers find that they are not yet ready for Circle Time. It is important that the whole-school Quality Circle Time model is in place to support Circle Time meetings. If this is not yet the case, it may be better to concentrate initially on the Golden Rules, Safety Routines and Golden Time. You are then developing a tried and tested incentive and sanction system which will give you a safer context within which to introduce Circle Time.

> When the implementation of these policies has created a calmer atmosphere, the time will be ripe to introduce Circle Time.

Acknowledgements
*Giving credits where
they are due!*

My tactful editor, Jo Browning Wroe, tentatively enquired as to how many pages I would be needing for this section (those of you who have read my previous acknowledgement pages may well share her fear!). Well – skip this part then – but this is the bit of the book I like the most! I write it when the main 'body' is nearly finished, the early mornings scribblings have ceased and the feeling of pressure has eased. I sit down with a strong sweet cup of tea and reflect on the really good things in life ... and people's kind faces shine through.

Help with the book

This year is the 'swan-song' for Helen Sonnet. She has been mentioned in all my previous books. She has been magnificent; she knows me and my way of working very well and this time she has taken away some creative sections and written them by herself. Thank you Helen.

Scotland

I've grown to love Scotland. One of the best aspects of my work has been discovering the beauty of this country and the clear vision of its educators. I admire many features of their education system – and the fact that OFSTED inspections haven't taken their toll on teachers' energy and morale. I am particularly grateful to David Cameron and Gordon Lennox for supporting a continuing programme of Training the Trainers. They do it with such style, real thoughtfulness – and a fund of wickedly funny stories.

My students

I still teach five modules on the M. Ed. for Bristol University. Each year I decide I just can't fit it in, but when it comes down to it I just can't resist the prospect of meeting the new wave of experienced teachers, many from different cultures, who learn enthusiastically but also give me so much back. They have all added to the 'circle', Last year my Indian teachers reminded me vividly of the importance of including meditation and visualisations within the circle … and this year the Dominican teachers have brought dance and songs to our Circle Time. Even though there are so many I could thank I need to single out Urmila Ramakrishna and Fiona Apperly. Their commitment, erudition and enthusiasm for the circle approach has been inspiring. They both have quiet calmness and sensitivity, a true sense of friendship and a deep love of children. I will follow their careers with great interest. I would also like to thank the students who have researched and completed many excellent assignments and dissertations on Circle Time in many different cultural contexts.

My team on the road

There is so much I could say! I have a team of specialist accredited consultants. There are other people I have accredited in the model who work for LEAs; but these are the only people who are entitled to promote this particular model for my consultancy. They are Margaret Goldthorpe, Maggie Grayson, Anna-Michele Hantler, Ann Topping, Therese Hoyle and Marilyn Tew … and they are brave!

Initially they all attended one of my residential training weeks and/or the M. Ed., they've shadowed me across the country, they've voluntarily piloted aspects of the model in their local schools and now are called in to support many different types of schools with a wide range of needs, hopes and fears. They don't always get the support that they deserve from me. I often don't practice what I preach, despite good intentions, like everyone else I get ambushed. So, forgive me, my valiant band, your challenges have been enormous, but I have wonderful testimonials from grateful schools, and consistently excellent evaluations from them.

My team at home

They have the worst job! They don't get happy smiles from circles of children, letters of thanks from schools, or evaluation sheets to read in order to remember the good times … they just get the frazzled woman they've heard *can*

viii   *MORE QUALITY CIRCLE TIME*

be full of energy and joie-de-vivre. Huh! Poor Ginny, Karen and Kim endlessly typing away, answering phones and emptying bins whilst life rages around them and my teenagers hang their washing on the 'office' radiators! You are real troupers – and at least 'that dog' has gone on a long holiday to my mum. Thank you.

Supporters

I've been very lucky this year. I've had many 'boosts' of real support for this model. I am full of respect for the following people. They share one thing in common; they are all busy yet they all make time to either help out or write lines of encouragement or offer valuable suggestions. Briefly, they are; Anita Roddick for sponsoring independent research; Simon Richey, who as assistant director of the Caloste Gulbenkian Foundation, continually gives encouragement and has sponsored a development of this model in secondary schools; Mo Mowlam who took time to write an endorsement of my work in Belfast schools; Lord David Putnam, who gave time to speak at the Quality Circle Time conference; Joanne Foster, Chair BT Forum, for her enthusiasm and good ideas; Nick Peacey, (SENJIT), for continuing to put on indepth training courses for his London teachers; Titus Alexander, (Self-Esteem Network), who continues to always be there when I am worried and keeps on flagging up the larger vision; Edward Lea (I've now got a business plan!); James Park, Director of Antidote who helped host a recent conference; Clive James, a man of amazing talent and energy; Georgia Thorpe who is determined we should get on the Web ...

... there are truly too many to mention. Even now I can see the wan face of Jo, who must be wondering how she can draw on all her usual sensitive, insightful, special skills to tell me that this section has to be cut. (Jo, when we have all our 'businessy – book wrangles', I keep a firm picture of our real respect and appreciation for each other which will always triumph over editorial decisions!

Our educators

... there are centres of glowing, peaceful excellence out there in our oft-tired, rushing country. These are schools who have worked incredibly hard to create this golden calm and I celebrate them. There are also LEAs peopled by wonderful educators who refuse just to firefight but have true vision. These people recognise there are no 'quick fixes' – only a long programme of steady Inset; Planning, Doing and Reviewing.

This year SENJIT from London University/Antidote and Self-Esteem Network hosted a London conference exclusively on this Whole School Quality Circle Time model. Children, lunchtime supervisors and teachers, many of whom have been working on the model for twelve years, from different parts of England, gave workshops for the conference.

A big 'Thank You' to everyone. The biggest credit of all must go to my friends, family and Curt, who put up with the fact that my passion for this work takes too much of my time away from them – yet they still remain loving and forgiving.

Foreword

Quality Circle Time –
the heart of the curriculum

At the moment, target-setting is the major issue under discussion. The obsession is to find fairer, but inevitably more exacting, ways of measuring attainment. The processes become more and more byzantine. I recently had one of the Scottish Office statisticians attempt to explain to me how the attainment targets for secondary schools had been calculated. When he mentioned polynomial equations as being essential in the calculation of the regression line, my eyes began to water. When he reeled off the letters and squares and 'to the powers of', I was biblical in my weeping. Of course, I want attainment to improve. Of course, I believe in having rigour in any form of evaluation or target-setting, but I fear that what should be a tool is becoming an obsession.

Sally Brown, professor of education at Stirling University, has directed us to the reality that nothing ever grew because it was measured. We need to look at how schools grow and how children grow within schools and to do so we have to look to emotional education and development, in the widest sense. We need to look at the issues surrounding emotional education and we need to look at case studies and models to see how we can make progress in supporting children's development.

Education conservatism

There is, undoubtedly, conservatism in education – despite the sense of frenetic change which so many teachers have. There is still a fear of losing control, and a feeling of needing to maintain authority over pupils. There is still a sense that the curriculum is almost more important than the child. The child must reach standards, must match attainment targets, must correspond to norms which are set by standardisation. This is not a culture which generates creativity or adaptability, the two key qualities required in the world as we experience it. It is not a culture which encourages balance or well-being or self-esteem. Sadly, it is not even a culture which generates high attainment. To seek the norm, to follow the well-trodden path, is to discover conformity and mediocrity. To emphasise scores and attainment is to encourage knowledge but to risk the loss of understanding.

Happily, it is a culture which is widely defied and subverted. We are fortunate in the quality of so much of the research which is conducted in this country and the quality of the researchers who carry it out. This takes us back, time and time again, to the centrality of the teaching and learning process. The four key elements in promoting effectiveness are identified as:

- the skills of the teacher, particularly in classroom management;
- aspirations and expectations;
- the morale of teaching staff and their attitude towards their craft;
- the readiness of schools to be dynamic – to look at what happens in classrooms, reflect on it and implement judicious change.

The IQEA research carried out by Dr David Hopkins in 1991 identified 'authentic relationships in the classroom as the key determinant of whether or not children would achieve'.

Work such as this takes us back into an examination of the classroom and an examination of the processes of learning as well as of its outcomes. We are blessed in the quality of many of the practitioners who work in our schools. We often do them a great disservice. It sometimes appears that we are only interested in celebrating the exceptional and idiosyncratic educators.

When we are not engaged in praising the exceptional, we seem to be equally readily caught up in the denigration of the weak teachers who let children down. I suspect these almost rival the former category in their rarity. What we fail to do is to celebrate the sound, capable teacher who performs an incredibly complex task well. Yet it is these teachers – who think about their pupils, who plan for their individual needs as far as possible, who respect their pupils and their colleagues – who make a difference to what happens to children. It is they who add value. Like those who conduct the overwhelming body of research, they understand that learning is a complex business and that it works when children have high aspirations and expectations of themselves. They realise that children need to be secure before they can learn effectively, that they have to be able to relate to others before they can relate to learning.

We can see this reflected in practice in countless classrooms where teachers work to establish a climate for learning before they concern themselves about their pupils' progress along whatever path of attainment has been set for them. We can see it on the innumerable occasions when teachers stop to respond to the stresses and needs of individual youngsters, knowing that progress is impossible unless their emotional upset is resolved.

The challenge to common sense

All of this makes sense. Sadly, sense – particularly common sense – has become a casualty of the highly polarised debate which seems to dog education at the moment. If that debate were remade as a film, it would be directed by Sergio Leone and Chris Woodhead, and the lead would be played by Clint Eastwood, who would be peering through narrowed eyes at Lee Van Cleef in the role of Michael Barber – that is, if he had survived an earlier shoot-out with Tim Brighouse (played by a miraculously resurrected Gary Cooper). It is, after all, a sort of intellectual *High Noon*.

In this debate, it is easy to caricature the leading figures, but it is equally easy to characterise and to caricature the viewpoints. Child centredness is left, soft and antithetical to achievement. It lacks rigour. It is outdated, permissive, demoralising, in the true sense of the word. In the language of George Orwell, 'curriculum good, child centredness bad'. This is an impossible climate in which to conduct productive discussion. It makes education a side-show where competing demonologies battle pointlessly one against the other.

It does not have to be this way. We can have synthesis as opposed to thesis and antithesis. We can have structure, we can have rigour and still have flexibility for and responsiveness to children. We can recognise the importance of personal development and still drive towards higher standards of academic attainment. We can have higher hopes of achieving these higher standards if we recognise the importance of personal development. We can care unashamedly about where our children come from, about who they are, and still maintain high expectations of them.

The contribution of Quality Circle Time

The Quality Circle Time model represents a very valid and valuable case study in how the needs of children can be given priority within a framework which is genuinely educational. Quality Circle Time deals with the creation of a learning culture by recognising children's need for self-esteem – in simpler terms, for a sense of worth. It is, in this sense, intrinsically child centred and, being so, can be classed as part of some sort of woolly, liberalist approach ready to derail the train of progress. This is not the message of research conducted on either side of the border. Work done in Scotland and in England, for once, gives the same message.

Staff morale and children's self-esteem are critical to success in learning. Without these there can be no such thing as school effectiveness. Neither can be created through an occasional dip into the odd strategy or session which aims to empower children. Such piecemeal approaches only serve to confuse young people. What they, and their teachers, require is an approach which is holistic. It must be rooted in research, drawing on the full range of educational knowledge. It must take account of how we think and how we learn. Without such roots, no development can be credible. It must impinge on the whole way in which a school works. It must provide a structure which is simple, but which pervades all that happens in a school.

I believe that this is what the Quality Circle Time model offers. It provides a basis for all aspects of the school's life. This is the essence of the Golden Rules approach, which recognises that we need only a simple code of conduct to allow schools to function. This code must be simple, and it must be adhered to and reinforced constantly. Those of us who are, or who have been, teachers know this. We have begun our time with a class by setting out the ground rules for our rooms. How much more valuable and productive it is to have the rules there, agreed and applicable, across the whole school. The larger and more complex the school is, the more essential is this approach. In that, the aims of the school are seen as the essential foundation for progress. Every school is encouraged to have a vision of itself and of where it wants to take its pupils. These aims are the basis for evaluating progress.

Teachers have, in very many instances, asked themselves what framework of rules they need to set to ensure that these aims are achieved, what kind of values must exist in their educational community to fulfil their vision. Quality Circle Time for staff can focus on this kind of discussion, clarifying for teachers what the school's aims are and how they translate into action.

Such discussion often needs the discipline and security which Circle Time offers. We are not always open to that sort of discussion otherwise and can be too quick to seek refuge behind cynicism, humour or the simple, but obstinate refusal to make eye contact. Importantly, Quality Circle Time stresses the need to involve all members of a school community in this sort of discussion and in the delivery of its outcomes.

There is an obvious tendency in this kind of presentation to sound like some demented Lancelot returning with the Holy Grail, but there is an element of benign synthesis in Quality Circle Time which at least approaches 'Grail' status. It puts in place communication across the school among pupils and staff. It provides values and a system of sanctions and incentives which promote these values in both the classroom and the playground. Children crave this consistency, as do staff. What it contributes beyond that is a monitoring mechanism to ensure that the structures are always under review. Both children and staff can comment, in the circle, on how the structure works.

It has huge attractions in allowing all children to be involved in discussions which promote peer support and self-discipline. It links also to what we know about how children develop understanding by using what they know and the skills that they have. It builds on these by recognising the very particular needs of children with real behavioural difficulty. The subsequent therapeutic approach to children 'beyond' provides an element of support which, increasingly, all schools need.

I have done enough training and been involved in enough ice breakers to have evaluated myself many times. Like most Scots, I have a strong element of pragmatism. I support what has been seen to work. This has been a powerful springboard in the adoption of Quality Circle Time in Scotland. Staff can refer to publications which offer a rationale alongside practical guidance. They have a permanent resource. They also have a model which can be demonstrated and which is so disciplined that they can then apply it.

It shows weaknesses when, as in other models, it becomes an occasion, an isolated part of the life of the school, a departure from the norm. It shows its strengths when it transcends that and operates across a learning community.

I am not suggesting that there are no other ways, no other models that offer the same potential. What I can record is that we have a majority of primary schools who are implementing this model. This is not in a uniform way, nor is it always proving effective. In all, however it is generating improvement. It is creating a situation where staff have to learn to talk to each other about their practice and about the way in which they relate to children. They are having to discuss what is important to them and to their school and having to try to agree on that. This is a step of enormous significance in itself.

Training the trainers – a crucial strategy for quality?

Quality Circle Time can also provide an important bridge between the education authority and its schools. In the case of Fife Council, we have committed ourselves to a programme of accredited training for the trainers within the council who can support and develop the Quality Circle Time model. This shows the extent to which we wish to emphasise the importance of quality and rigour. It also emphasises the extent to which we wish to highlight the importance of relationships. It underscores the way in which we share the concerns and values of our teachers. Finally, it ensures the integrity of the model within our schools. We believe this strategy is vital to its success.

To sum up

In all of our schools it is providing a set of values which are simple, which relate to their school aims and which begin to define their institutions as learning communities. They are finding increased clarity about what is important in making their schools work. For many young people it is providing a way of relating which is new to them, but to which they can adapt quickly and well.

I have been moved to see and hear what happens when children have Circle Time. I have heard them acknowledge problems, and weaknesses, and then heard others offer constructive ways of helping and supporting them. I love to hear that replicated, in the best examples, in other areas of their work, in language or mathematics. It changes the patterns of relationships and therefore addresses chronic problems like bullying and victimisation. In particular, it can offer opportunities to assist boys by bringing them in to a safe area for communication and exchange, something which girls seem more adept at carving out for themselves.

This enthusiasm is not the zeal of the converted. It is a very genuine response from someone who spends much of his time trying to encourage individual teachers and schools to weave together their many threads of excellent practice and see for themselves the very fine garment which they have. That all too often is our problem, not the lack of quality but the failure to recognise it and strengthen it with coherence. I saw much of what I did instinctively reflected in the Quality Circle Time model, but in a framework which gave it an academic rationale and a powerfully holistic structure. I would argue that is what all of us need now in education: not new models or – worse – enforced changes, but those models which reflect our own best practice back to us in a new light which shows its strengths and gives us ways in which we can improve on them.

I feel that in Quality Circle Time most of us can see that sort of reflection; one which clarifies the need for vision for our schools and for values which support that vision. It reinforces the need for pupils to have self-esteem and for practical strategies which, in a simple way, translate all of these into something which can make a real difference for our young people.

David Cameron,
Quality Performance Review Manager,
Fife City Council, Scotland

References: see Appendix 2.

Preface

Do we really need another book on Circle Time?

Why am I writing yet another Circle Time book?

My first slim volume, *All Round Success*, was written in the mid-1980s with a team of teachers for Wiltshire Education Authority. It was followed in the early 1990s by a large management manual, *Turn Your School Round*, and in 1996 by the comprehensive, *Quality Circle Time*. This Circle Time 'stable' has been added to subsequently by one of my valued team of consultants, Margaret Goldthorpe, with her *Effective IEPs Through Circle Time* (1998) and, even more recently, her *Poems for Circle Time and Literacy Hour*. In addition, during this period I helped to develop LDA's *Self-Esteem Builders*, a range of resources designed to support the Quality Circle Time model; and I have just created the *Quality Circle Time Kit* with essential props to ensure that the approach maximises its creative potential.

Throughout this period, due to my early work in counselling work with women, my friend Eileen Gillibrand and I have written other resources to help women maintain morale and energy. *She Who Dares Wins* (1995) and *When I Go to Work I Feel Guilty* (1997), both with a foreword by Anita Roddick, have been published by HarperCollins. Maybe people have really had enough now? Certainly many people on the hundreds of courses I have run in the UK have often asked how I maintain the interest and energy to continue to write and drive around the country giving thousands of workshops. The simple answer is **passion**. I think that feeling passionately about your work, if it synthesises your values and beliefs into practical strategies, can give you enormous drive. I know that Circle Time has given back to many teachers a joy in teaching that has penetrated all the efforts of the rest of their lives. The Body Shop recently funded a report commissioned by Wiltshire Local Education Authority on the use of Circle Time in Wiltshire primary schools. Headteachers were asked various questions about the value of Circle Time in their schools. Below are some of their comments:

> *"I believe Circle Time (and its underlying premises) has permeated everything we do, including classroom activities, staff meetings (teaching and non-teaching) and even governors' meetings."*

> *"[Circle Time] provides opportunities to tackle difficult behaviours and in small group work can provide an opportunity for shy, quiet children to find their voice."*

> *"Despite its success in our school, I think the major factor about Circle Time is that the children LOVE it – it's a chance in a busy world to have time to speak!"*

> *"It helps in mixing the sexes and social groups and removes barriers that quite often start to develop. It allows children and shows them that it is safe to share their feelings with people they trust. It leads them to being confident in approaching an adult about worries and concerns (home and school)."*

One hundred percent of the headteachers who took part in the survey agreed that Circle Time helps children to understand, know and value other people. This continuing wave of enthusiasm inspires us all to keep going!

I do try really hard to practice what I preach and I build in Golden Moments and adhere to a weekly Personal Care Plan (page 26) although I don't always manage it!

A classic example of the guru being 'unseated' occurred recently after the publication of my second self-help book for women, *When I Go to Work I Feel Guilty*. I had been invited to give an interview on Radio 4 and at 5.30 in the morning was groggily making preparations to leave the house. Tip-toeing along the landing, I happened to glance into the hamster's cage and noticed that Colin seemed unusually comatose. A closer inspection left me doubting that he was in a state of hibernation and, not wishing to confront that difficult situation at that precise moment, I hastily covered him over with more cotton-wool bedding.

The interview was conducted through a link between myself in Bristol and the presenter in London. I was basking in the glory of my recent success and waxing lyrical on the worthy philosophies contained in my book when the presenter suddenly introduced, on air, an editor who was armed to the teeth with statistics supporting her argument that women should stay at home with their children. Faced with such an unexpected ambush, all my own sound advice on dealing with situations like this evaporated. I panicked. My answers deteriorated to stuttered responses. The final agony arrived when the editor directed a question relating to children's well-being at me. My mind raced to produce the appropriate response. Out it came. 'In order to raise happy healthy hamsters one needs to ...'. My fate was sealed. My daughters, who were listening in and recognise a Freudian slip when they hear one, raced upstairs to examine Colin. How are the mighty fallen!

However, in spite of my failures, I remain convinced of the real value in my life and the lives of others of the philosophy behind Quality Circle Time and my enthusiasm never wavers! Nothing compensates for independent training, but this self-help manual will go a long way towards helping.

References: see Appendix 2.

SECTION 1

Understanding the model

Circle Time gives back to many teachers a joy in learning

Why has this grassroots Circle Time movement spread so rapidly? Basically, teachers are good-hearted people who have felt, over the years, that they were merely pushing children through academic hoops. Circle Time ensured that they could allow children a time to 'come forward', unfettered by labels or academic failure. The safety of the circle meant that they could just be themselves; a raggedy collection of individuals struggling to find more honest and respectful ways of going forward. It was a time of the week when respect, integrity and courage really mattered and children could be celebrated for their qualities of calmness, kindness and honesty. It gave classes a sense of shared community. However …

Quality Circle Time is a vulnerable model

Because the model involves people, it is vulnerable. At its worst, it can be misused by teachers who try to 'shame' children publicly into behaving. At its mediocre level, it can become boring and repetitive. At its best, it can be uplifting for children … but may be very worrying for them when they leave its emotionally safe confines to re-enter other school areas where the adults bicker or engage in unkind behaviour. Then they quietly note that there is a huge chasm between the apparent 'caring' demonstrated in Circle Time and what actually happens outside. They become demoralised and lose faith in the displayed moral values. They can see that these values are neither vibrant nor dynamic – they are being used merely as a control mechanism.

Emotionally and physically exhausted teachers are prey to negativity

There is no doubt that the current climate of constant change, inspection and target-setting has taken its toll on the national psyche of teachers. Self-esteem is very low in many individuals, bringing a growing sense of inadequacy, guilt and anxiety. Research has proved (Burns 1982) that teachers with high self-esteem foster high self-esteem pupils, who are then able to fulfil a high academic potential. Teachers with low self-esteem can sink into worrying patterns of nagging, bullying and inconsistent behaviour. Our own research reveals that the part of the Quality Circle Time model that is most underused is Circle Time for adults. I feel this is partly because teachers find it hard to justify creating special time for themselves, partly because in some instances they're afraid that certain strong personalities on their staff may sabotage their efforts.

Until the adults feel emotionally safe with each other, excellence cannot be released. People will only say or do what is safe, rather than risk trying something new which might fail and not be supported by other members of staff. It is pointless trying to promote this model in schools if adults themselves won't work on their personal and professional development.

The false divide between behaviour and PSE

Our education system is riddled with false divides. The most serious is the divide between PSE and behaviour. In the UK we have a range of 'positive behaviour models' and Personal and Social (PSE) models – and separate policies for both. The two are indivisible. Internalising moral values is the key to both policies – and 'relationships' is the bridge between the two. We have to explore the relationship between ourselves and others, and empathy is the quality that has to be unlocked. Only if people understand and care about other people's inner worlds will they modify their behaviour.

I believe we can only teach the syllabus of PSE (e.g. drugs, hygiene, smoking) after the teacher and the classes have worked on creating a classroom community committed to working on their relationships. Circle Time is team building. Only when the team is safe with each other, can you introduce challenging, potentially devisive subjects such as drugs, hygiene, sex, etc.

The Quality Circle Time model is becoming diluted through lack of indepth training

At present, teachers do not receive proper training, and many LEA-support personnel attend only a one-day course and then go back and deliver their own courses on this model through their LEA Inset programme. Consequently, it becomes diluted and, because its underpinning pedagogy has never been fully explored by the trainer, Circle Time can become merely a superficial cosmetic gesture. Teachers attending such courses receive second-hand ideas, then take them back to their schools and the children receive third and fourth hand knowledge! (See Resources section for details of accredited training.) Because 'Circle Time' is a trendy new buzzword, many schools put it in their policies and on their timetables, but they don't know enough about its psychology, its structures and its ground rules and therefore fail to realise its potential. Worse than that, in many cases the schools fail to act on the listening systems; they fail to incorporate many of the management issues raised by children into their subsequent action plans. Very soon children 'smell' the hypocrisy and become aware of a further divide between values and action and can pull back from participating.

What Quality Circle Time is not

- ○ It is not just sitting round in a circle; it is a whole-school model that concerns itself with every moment of a child's day.
- ○ It is timetabled – you don't just have Circle Time because you have had a fight in the playground.
- ○ It is not a Quick Fix to difficult behaviour – it is a long process of Plan-Do-Review.
- ○ It is not just a newsround of what's gone on over the weekend.
- ○ It is not about getting disclosures – personal issues are taken to the other two listening systems.
- ○ It is not games just for the sake of games.
- ○ It is not just a chat.
- ○ It is not all about being nice to each other on cue – one person saw a Circle Time where all the children had to say something nice about each other and one poor child was told off loudly because they could not think of anything nice to say!

References: see Appendix 2.

The value of the Quality Circle Time model

The world is becoming increasingly emotionally dysfunctional and uncertain for everyone. Children require greater support than ever in establishing a clear sense of themselves and a capacity to relate respectfully to others. This is vital in terms of their ability to learn to achieve their academic and social potential in school, as well as being an essential part of their preparation for life. The Quality Circle Time model meets these needs. Children require consistency and respect in the way they are treated within the school community; they need a sense of being safe and being supported, whilst still being empowered to make choices and to state their views.

This model is based on respect for the whole person – child, teacher, support staff or parent. It does not focus just on behaviour but enables people to deal with underlying factors that cause poor behaviour and result in low achievement.

It aims to create an upward spiral of energy by focusing on the well-being and morale of staff as much as of children and parents, thereby relieving stress and raising self-esteem among adults in order that they have enough stamina to raise the self-esteem of young people.

Through regular timetabled Circle Time meetings for all adults and children, emotional and physical space is created for every member of the school community to speak and to be heard, thereby developing citizenship, participation and a sense of community.

It is a tried and tested model, which is being used in thousands of schools and which has been evaluated by practising teachers, praised in hundreds of OFSTED reports and validated by an independent research team at Bristol University.

What sets this model apart?

How can you help people want to become responsible citizens rather than to be 'managed' into good behaviour?

There are three main elements which distinguish this model from all others.

❶ It encompasses the demand for rigour by providing a highly structured, but simple approach. It has firm recommendations for all aspects of a school day. It has policies for staff morale, moral value systems, an incentive and sanction system, a lunchtime policy and a structured behavioural and therapeutic approach for children 'beyond' the normal motivational strategies. It also uses the circle to support teachers who are themselves under unacceptable levels of stress.

❷ Once all the structures are in place, the Circle Time meetings continue to act as their own review body to assess their effectiveness, as a proactive system to deal with any new problems, and as a forum for the continuing promotion of values, positive relationships and the community celebration of success. When these structures are well established, all Circle Times can be connected by 'bridges' which are crossed back and forth by a person responsible for taking any information affecting the running of the school to a further appropriate circle. In this way, the whole school community is able to speak and listen to each other. School councils can be run as Circle Times and adult representatives from all sections of the school community, including two children from each class, can discuss management issues raised in class Circle Times.

❸ Unlike any other behaviour management model, this model provides a forum in which children can learn supported self-discipline and moral development. It therefore has a huge impact on building peer support and diminishing bullying. Whilst it also has the key features of any sound behavioural system – ie original suggestions for sanctions and incentives and lunchtimes – it uses the weekly Circle Time to help children develop empathy, respect and responsibility towards others. Eventually they *want* to be responsible citizens rather than need to be 'managed' into good behaviour.

Can Circle Time contribute to emotional intelligence?

The concept of multiple intelligences has grown in stature over recent years following the rigorous research carried out by Howard Gardner (1993). Daniel Goleman (1996) added even greater credibility with his best-selling book, *Emotional Intelligence*. Their school of thought considers that 'learning' in the academic sense involves one type of intelligence, but others are needed in order for us to lead successful and happy lives in society. These have been divided into five main areas, namely:

> **knowing one's emotions,**
> **managing one's emotions,**
> **motivating oneself,**
> **recognising emotions in others,**
> **handling relationships.**

Relating to others

Until recently, our education system has relied too heavily on developing the cognitive domain, neglecting the common-sense awareness, that what really helps people to succeed in life is not their collection of academic qualifications but their skill in relating to others. We all know people who have no GCSEs, but whose ability to manage their own and others' lives is strikingly insightful and organised. These people have gifts of sensitivity, empathy, conflict resolution, assertiveness and humour, and a readiness to praise and accept praise. Our work with the Quality Circle Time model has proved that, whilst some people own these qualities naturally, it is possible to teach everyone relationship skills. Self-esteem theory teaches us that if a person is treated with respect and warmth, 'the individual will see himself as having the characteristics and values that others attribute to him'. (Rogers 1961)

If we perceive ourselves as likeable, good company, worthy of being listened to and so on, we then act towards others as if we have those attributes, thereby creating a positive self-fulfilling prophecy.

Circle Time provides the ideal opportunity for all our intelligences to be stretched and challenged. Children are not only specifically taught the skills they need for personal and social development, but they also learn self-awareness and how to recognise and monitor their own feelings. In addition, they are taught strategies to handle their and others' feelings in a respectful and sensitive way. They become self-motivated through an understanding of the benefits and freedom that develop from being able to regulate their own responses and take charge of their own destinies. Circle Time places great emphasis on the need for empathy, for understanding another's world, and helps the children to explore and discover successful ways of interacting with others.

Today's educators are calling out for schools to explore models that lay the foundation for emotional education. Education Minister Estelle Morris called for schools to practise the 'Fourth R' – that is, 'relationships'.

The *Initial Report on Education for Citizenship and the Teaching of Democracy in Schools* (1998) asked the question:

> **So what do we mean by 'effective education for citizenship?' ... Firstly, children learning from the very beginning self-confidence and socially and morally responsible behaviour both in and beyond the classroom, both towards those in authority and each other.**

Certainly, the Quality Circle Time model, with its all-inclusive policies, involves parents and all relevant agencies. Not only do all of these receive copies of the Golden Rules, but they also work on their own ground rules of respect through the programme of circle meetings we advise schools to initiate for the whole school community. We believe that children will more easily become responsible citizens once they, themselves, have played a part in creating a socially responsible, democratically run community within the classroom. Once they have experienced the benefits of mutual respect they will be motivated to recreate these values in their future homes and "outside" communities.

The Social Exclusion Unit (1998), **in their report on truancy and social exclusion, 1998, drew attention to the fact that:**

> **Children can become disaffected when school seems boring, too difficult or unlikely to lead anywhere. Many schools and other agencies lack the training, support or simply time to get to grips with what are very difficult problems.**

A commitment by schools to this model is a commitment to making the time to grapple with the problems and issues. One of the strongest psychological theories influencing the development of this model is Maslow's hierarchy of needs (Maslow 1962, 1970). He postulated that individuals have a need for physiological well-being, safety, a sense of belonging and positive self-esteem and only when they have them can they realise their inner creative potential through a process he called 'self-actualisation', or realising their inner potential. Only when schools and agencies work together on a programme of timetabled Circle Time meetings regulated by firm imperatives for respect for each other can they say that they have the child's emotional needs at the heart of all they are doing.

If we were to unravel all the above issues in a much longer academic thesis, we would inevitably come to the conclusion that emotional education, self-esteem and academic achievement are not only interlinked; they are indivisible.

For years now educational commentators have been voicing these same concerns. **Purkey, 1970, nearly thirty years ago, wrote**:

> **students' failures in basic subjects, as well as the misdirected motivation and lack of commitment characteristic of the under-achiever ... are in large measure the consequence of faulty perceptions of themselves and the world ... the overwhelming body of contemporary research points insistently to the relationship between self-esteem and academic achievement ...**

It is extraordinary that, in the nineties, we are still having to justify, in education a broader understanding of the nature of intelligence. Any historical study of philosophy, psychology and the related sciences will reveal a number of passionate educators making the same case.

Perhaps the last word should go to Krishnamurti:

> *"We must be very clear in ourselves what we want, clear what a human being must be – the total human being ...*

If we concentrate very much on examinations, on technological information, on making the child clever, proficient in acquiring knowledge, while we neglect the other side, then the child will grow up into a one sided human being. When we talk about a total human being, we mean not only a human being with inward understanding, with a capacity to explore, to examine his inward being, his inward state and the capacity of going beyond it, but also someone who is good in what he does outwardly. The two must go together. That is the real issue in education – to see that when the child leaves the school, he is well established in goodness, both outwardly and inwardly ... By giving your heart to years of acquiring knowledge you have already destroyed something in you – the feeling and the capacity to look. By emphasising one or the other you become insensitive and the essence of intelligence is sensitivity."

(J Krishnamurti, 1974)

It is therefore vital that teachers – like you, the reader – embark on a journey towards the synthesis of the above ideas with courage and rigour. With this aim in mind, we have constructed self-evaluation checklists (see pages 24–49).

In the absence of the ideal of direct training, self-training must be the answer.

Reference: see Appendix 2.

3 The model at a glance

THE JENNY MOSLEY WHOLE-SCHOOL QUALITY CIRCLE TIME MODEL DEVELOPED 1986–1999

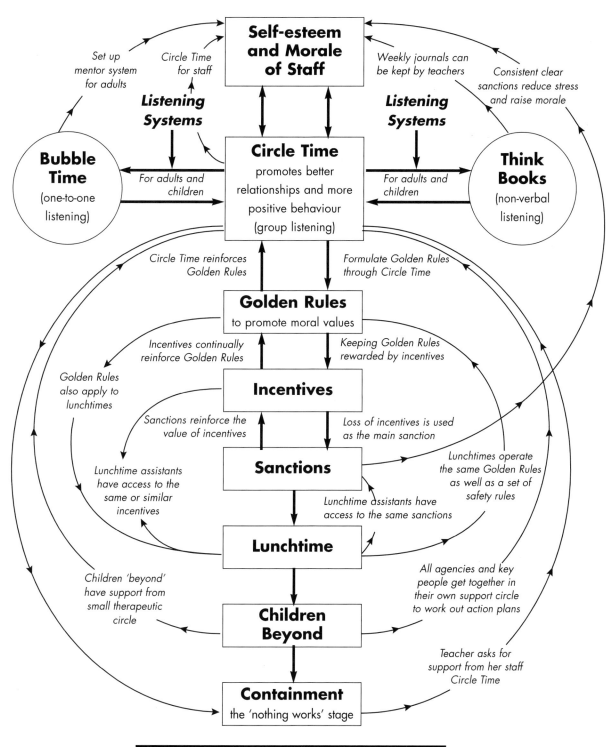

AN ECOSYSTEMIC MODEL

4 Unravelling the model

The Jenny Mosley Whole-School Quality Circle Time model, developed 1986–1998

Self-esteem and morale of staff

In this model the first focus is on the mental health of all the adults. It is impossible to expect adults to respond positively, warmly and calmly to children if they themselves are emotionally and physically exhausted and/or lacking in team spirit or support. All adults in the school community are seen as equal in their ability to affect each other positively or negatively. When possible, we include all ancillary and support staff and parents in our training. We teach a particular model of personal and professional care plans and a stress-reduction strategy called **Golden Moments**. We also explore a range of ground rules of respect that the adults can work on with each other. The emphasis is on personal responsibility – each one of us is responsible for looking after our own mental and physical health; and collective responsibility – we are all responsible for looking after each other.

Setting up the three listening systems

Quality Circle Time, a highly structured group-listening system, is timetabled weekly for children and monthly for adults. For children, the Circle Time rules and strategies enable them to practise and participate in relationship education. You cannot 'teach' children moral values; they must experience them. All the games and exercises are designed to build up a sense of 'class community'; once this safe boundary is established children can then engage in activities specifically chosen to promote the values upheld by the Golden Rules; see *Quality Circle Time* (Mosley 1996), where the underlying moral value for each Circle Time meeting is clearly stated. In addition to establishing Circle Time as a class-listening system to which other adults can be invited, the school also sets up one-to-one listening systems referred to as **Bubble Time** in primary schools, (see *Quality Circle Time*) and **Talk Time** in secondary schools. In addition, we introduce a daily non-verbal listening system, **Think Books**. The adults commit themselves to working on their personal and professional development by engaging in their own regular Circle Times. In other words, timetabled listening is placed at the heart of the school. Firm structures and ground rules are taught to participants to maintain emotional 'safety' and to promote specific relationship skills.

Incentives

The reward system again has been structured to reinforce the moral values – the Golden Rules. All the words on the stickers and certificates are chosen to echo the words highlighted in the rules; for example, **Well done for being gentle/being kind/being honest/ being positive towards other people**. These rewards are given to the whole school community in order that they can all congratulate each other – including lunchtime supervisors, caretakers and children. In this way the system is highly democratic and the underlying moral principle, all members of a community are equally important and all are entitled to be respected and valued, is demonstrated. Circle Time is used as the specific forum through which children and adults can take time to show appreciation and congratulate each other, both verbally and through the awarding of incentives.

Sanctions

The sanction system, also linked to the Golden Rules, is based on the creation of a weekly privilege entrusted to all children. If they break the Golden Rules, a visual warning such as a sad face or a large W is placed beside them; if they choose to break another rule whilst the warning is in place they lose a small slot of Golden Time. This system has proved to be extremely successful – it can even work in schools for emotionally and behaviourally disturbed children; many head-teachers will testify to its power. The reason for its success is that the privileges chosen are individual, highly motivational and often community based (e.g. older classes pair with a younger class; one privilege is to teach a younger child). This deceptively simple system is powerful precisely because it forms part of the incentive system. All the children who behave well (the 'middle plodders') receive their just entitlement, (weekly privileges) and all those who keep to the Golden Rules for a full half-term automatically receive a special Golden Certificate. All the adults in the school community can use this system (as can the children in relation to each other) and all the parents are notified about how it works and what to expect. Participation in this system helps children to learn that communities are prepared to put time and effort into upholding their moral values.

Lunchtime policy

Many children's behavioural problems (and many school discipline problems) stem from the fact that they do not know how to play with each other. We have a generation of imaginatively and socially impoverished children due to the growth of technology and the fact that our streets are not safe for children to learn and play games on. This policy insists that schools teach playground games as part of their PE syllabus. It zones the playground into activity areas supervised by older children who have applied and been interviewed for the job of 'lunchtime helper'. A community-service-type task force is formed for all children who need to be constructively occupied. Football parliaments are held in order to ensure that football contributes to the positive ethos of a school and does not pull against it. Lunchtime supervisors are given the same rights as teachers and are encouraged to use the same incentive and sanction system; they are also invited to regular Circle Time meetings with children and with members of staff. In this way lunchtimes are seen as part of the moral whole. When schools fail to offer these structures children inadvertently learn that moral values are only practised inside buildings with power. Unfortunately, they may then feel that their needs and the needs of other children are being ignored and that they are left to survive, in any way they can, in a barren wilderness.

'Children beyond'

This phrase is used to refer to children who are beyond being able to respond to or benefit from the normal proactive motivational procedures outlined in the model above. These children, due to their level of inner chaos and distress, need the security of three approaches, incorporating behavioural, therapeutic and peer support. A range of guaranteed success programmes and small achievable target systems is drawn up from within the support of class Circle Times. In addition, these children are offered the opportunity to attend **smaller therapeutic Circle Times**. It is at this stage that parents and other agencies are brought in to support and add to the approaches being used by the school. Once children see troubled children being offered this sort of support, they come to see the school as a moral community prepared to support and help its more disadvantaged members.

Containment

If all the methods outlined in the above model fail to help the 'child beyond', there is no more an ordinary main-stream school can offer. The focus of attention must now switch from the child to saving the sanity of the class teacher and all the other children in the class; otherwise a teacher can lose the vision of what teaching used to be like before the disturbed child arrived (and if teachers lose this vision, the teaching profession may lose highly skilled, experienced teachers through stress). It is at this stage that the **model becomes circular** – the teacher can take her need for support and help to the established monthly staff Circle Time, where the staff work out a written timetable of support. Meanwhile, the headteacher, safe in the knowledge there is no more the school can do to help that child, seeks a place in the smaller therapeutic community of a special needs school. The timetable of support enables the teacher to have a break every day and thus survive the period of time that it will take for the child to be placed in a setting that can meet their needs more appropriately.

The Whole-School Quality Circle Time model is successful because:

it establishes these strong and simple foundations:

- simple, structured approach
- easily implemented recommendations
- universally acceptable values template
- clear incentives and sanctions for all involved
- 'all embracing' holistic vision and process
- designed to support, not burden, teachers;

it has a continuous monitoring and evaluation system:

- staff and classes use the circle to review and assess their own progress
- proactive and creative ways are provided to deal with new problems
- celebration of success is integral
- individual class issues/solutions are cross-connected to other classes;

it promotes social development – 'results from within':

- children develop self-discipline
- children feel they are a valued part of a community and act accordingly
- children learn important mediation skills
- builds peer support and morale
- very positive impact on bullying and gang culture
- ultimately children create and respect, rather than adhere to, socially acceptable behaviour in their schools.

To sum up, the basic assumptions of Quality Circle Time are:

- The adults in school need to attend to their needs before they can attend to the children's.
- Individuals can only feel respected if they are heard, and their ideas acted upon.
- Children have within themselves the capacity to change their own behaviour.
- Individuals will only be motivated by abstract concepts such as democracy, citizenship, fairness etc, if these concepts are part of their "lived-in" reality.
- People enjoy helping each other.
- We all have the capacity to make clear choices in our lives – peer support can clarify these choices.
- Unless we are emotionally and physically safe we cannot learn, grow, or take risks which could lead us to "excellence".
- Fun is an important motivator.
- Negative behaviour is a result of unmet needs and responsible behaviour results from "met" needs.
- We all enjoy positive feedback and this good experience gives us the energy to want to recreate it for others.
- Many emotional and behavioural problems in schools are the result of the failure to put in proactive listening systems.
- We will never engender a sense of community until the classroom first becomes a democratic community.
- A good sanctions system can enhance self-esteem as it gives children safe boundaries and shows them that adults care about the values.

The values that underpin Quality Circle Time are:

Respect for self.
Respect for others.
Respect for our immediate and wider environment.

SECTION 2

Improving the quality of the model

Evaluating your practice through self-assessment

Quality Circle Time has many parts to it. It is easy for teachers to think they are running Circle Time well, but if vital pieces are missing, the vibrant image can never be complete.

We have created a series of evaluation sheets which will ensure that you have a clearer picture of where you are in the context of the model. The areas are discussed fully in *Turn Your School Round* (Mosley 1993) and *Quality Circle Time* (Mosley 1996). The format presented below has proved, in the absence of direct training by a specialist accredited in this model, to be a valuable self-help initiative.

One very helpful way to use the checklists is to have staff meetings focused on particular features of the Quality Circle Time Model. Individuals can complete the checklist and then have a round of, for example, '**I am pleased** because my children are really good at getting the class ready for Circle Time.' This could be followed by a round of, for example, 'I need to work on timetabling my Circle Times properly.'

Honesty is very important, and it will often be appropriate to discuss in the context of a Circle Time session with the children aspects of the model that need adjusting, or indeed to celebrate things that are going well.

The following are pointers in the right direction. They are not comprehensive. If you have any other ideas which you feel would help other colleagues and schools, please take a few minutes and send them to us. We'll incorporate them in subsequent new editions!

References: see Appendix 2.

LOOKING AFTER MYSELF IN SCHOOL

	Yes	No
Do I have some time during each day when I practise the philosophy of Golden Moments and give myself five stress-free minutes?		
Have I created enjoyable rituals with the pupils for the beginning and end of each day to help us feel calm and cheerful?		
Am I able to state my needs to colleagues in a pleasant but effective way?		
Do I use effective assertive strategies to deal with conflicts, thereby avoiding confrontation and tension?		
Do I make time to prioritise the work I need to tackle, rather than trying to complete everything at once?		
Am I able to recognise and deal with personal 'ambushes' effectively? In other words, do I recognise that some people hurt each other because of their own problems and that I do not need to take everything personally?		
Do I accept that the children and myself are allowed to make mistakes without feeling guilty?		
Do I eat properly and drink plenty of water throughout the day to maintain my energy levels?		
Do I ask for help and support from colleagues at crucial times?		
Do I have clear boundaries, e.g., do I go home at a designated time?		
Do I look after myself physically?		

	Yes	No
Do I take steps to maintain interest and enthusiasm in my work – e.g. attend courses, read current literature, try out new ideas, welcome fresh challenges?		
Am I able to recognise and celebrate my strengths? In other words, do I work on my own self-esteem?		

LOOKING AFTER MYSELF
OUT OF SCHOOL

	Yes	No
Am I able to let go of worries and concerns engendered through work? Do I need to practise 'creating boundaries' – i.e. definite switching-off times and rituals that signify the end of work and the beginning of leisure time?		
Do I have adequate rest and sleep?		
Do I have a balanced and healthy diet?		
Do I set aside regular time for personal enjoyment and pleasure?		
Do I maintain interests outside work through hobbies and pastimes?		
Do I enjoy a varied and fulfilling social life?		
Do I have sources of support?		
Do I take regular exercise to maintain my energy levels?		
Do I keep my mind active through reading, seeing plays, lively discussions etc.?		
Do I develop my spirituality through religion, nature, mysticism etc.?		
Do I give time to my friendships?		
Do I enjoy relaxing times with my family?		
Do I seek extra help to meet my needs? E.g., massage, therapy.		

LOOKING AFTER MY COLLEAGUES

	Yes	No
Could I suggest that we should have circle meetings for ourselves once a month?		
Could I suggest we have a staff social committee to organise half-termly social functions?		
Would I like to suggest that all the staff contribute funds to invite a yoga teacher to teach us relaxation techniques one lunchtime or after school? Or do I have a better idea for something we could all enjoy together?		
Could I suggest that we formulate Golden Rules for ourselves to put up in the staff room – e.g. listen well, don't interrupt, no moan without a suggestion for change, smile once a day?		
Could I suggest that we have a staff Golden Moment – e.g. a regular weekly lunch together with background music and no talk of difficult children?		
Could I suggest that we end each staff meeting with a celebratory round of 'one thing I achieved this week was'? (As opposed to one more thing I have to do.)		
Do I remember to thank colleagues for support or advice they have offered?		
Do I show that I recognise and value the strengths of my colleagues?		
Do I maintain professional behaviour towards colleagues – e.g. no back-biting about others, no passing on items of gossip?		
Do I find it easy to forgive colleagues if I feel they have done me an injustice?		
Do I apologise whenever I've been a 'pain' towards my colleagues or had an off day?		

QUALITY CIRCLE TIME MEETINGS

Before you can introduce Circle Time you need a calm, positive atmosphere. If your classroom suffers from a range of low level disruptive behaviours, first introduce the Golden Rules and the Golden Time. Once you have established the procedure of putting down warnings it is then possible to use the same incentives and sanctions within Circle Time. Sometimes, a laminated warning card placed by a child's feet in Circle Time saves you having to raise your voice and quickly restores order.

	Yes	No
Have I chosen a time of day for Circle Time that suits my energy level? Circle Time can be physically and mentally exhausting, so it is important that it is timetabled for a period when you are likely to be most alert and least stressed, e.g. immediately after lunch.		
Am I well organised when setting up the circle? Some teachers have reported that setting up the circle can be so problematic that they are often tempted to abandon Circle Time. There are two options for dealing successfully with this problem. Either responsible older children can organise a circle of chairs for a class during break/ lunchtime, or a class can be instructed in a well-ordered drill, complete with a wall plan showing where tables etc. should be placed. This can be fun; children can try to 'beat the clock', removing tables and creating a circle of chairs as quickly and efficiently as possible.		
Did I inform the children when it would be happening? Unless Circle Time is properly timetabled, at the same time each week, children will not trust or give themselves to it. It is a good idea to remind children a day or two before so that they can come to the circle in a state of readiness.		

	Yes	No
When the listening systems of Bubble Time, Think Books and Circle Time were set up, did I inform the children that, whilst I respect their privacy and right to confidentiality, anything they told me that was of a particularly worrying nature might have to be taken further? This is a very important consideration as you do not want a situation to arise in which a child considers you have betrayed their trust. If you don't have the other two systems set up children will be 'forced' to disclose in the circle. Remind the children that the circle is not the right place to say very personal things. It's best they have a quiet word with the teacher during Bubble Time or through their Think Books.		
Did I take a deep breath and create a positive focus before starting? Make sure you let go of all the day's problems before you start. You need to be free of these to concentrate on any issues and enjoy the fun element of Circle Time.		
Did I preface Circle Time with the skills the children needed to use? Briefly focus on the skills of 'thinking, looking, listening, speaking and concentrating' as a means of creating the right approach. Do this as a quick game by repeating the skills and at the same time pointing to head, eyes, ears, mouth, then sitting up straight and folding arms.		
Was the focus of my Circle Time appropriate for my class? Make sure that your sessions focus on issues relevant to your class, rather than keeping to a set programme which may not be addressing important and pertinent issues.		

	Yes	No

Was my circle session structured in the right way?
 	
It's very important to create the right balance between fun and serious issues and to adhere to a structure that sustains movement between these different elements. Ideally, Circle Time should include:
    ◐ starting game,
    ◐ round/follow-up activity,
    ◐ Open Forum,
    ◐ celebration of success,
    ◐ ending activity. (See *Quality Circle Time*.)		

Did I respond proactively to negative behaviour within the circle? Research has demonstrated that if you give a negative response to one child (e.g. 'Don't fidget – sit still'), you are likely to have to repeat this to many more children who note your response and then repeat the behaviour. It is far better to praise a child who is behaving well and sitting near the child whose behaviour is annoying you.		

Did I use effective encouragement with the children to help them keep the Circle Time rules?
 	
These include:
    ◐ praising specific children who are practising the social skills,
    ◐ giving out stickers which focus on positive behaviour,
    ◐ allowing time for children to praise each other,
    ◐ mentioning how the Golden Rules are incorporated into the activities.		

Did I follow a prearranged sanction system? Ideally this should be a verbal warning, then a visual warning symbol, and finally time out of the circle (5 minutes) measured using a timer.		

	Yes	No
Did I organise a facility for any child who did not respond to the normal sanctions above? It is a good idea to organise facilities with another teacher whereby a child could be removed to another classroom with prearranged work ready on the table ready for them to do.		
Did I provide an opportunity during Open Forum for children to nominate themselves for help with behaviour? This is important. It encourages whole-class support, which will increase the likelihood of success.		
Did I encourage shy children to participate? A good way to help shy children who may feel panicky when they are put 'on the spot' is to give advance warning (a day or two) of an item in Circle Time (e.g. a round of 'My favourite food is …') and ask the children to write down their responses on a card. If a child is still too shy to speak aloud, they can appoint someone else to read their card. Such a child may feel able to speak to a puppet held by the teacher.		
Were the children given the right to pass in a round and then reoffered the opportunity to speak? At the end of the round the child who started asks if any of the passes now want to speak. Children often gain confidence and ideas from listening as the rest of the class respond.		

Have I evaluated Circle Time with the children? ie. One thing I like about Circle Time … One thing I don't like about Circle Time …
 	
This helps to:
   ○ maintain the maximum potential of Circle Time,
   ○ avoid bad or sloppy practices creeping in,
   ○ keep up the pace of the sessions.		

	Yes	No
Have I followed up any matters arising from Circle Time? It is not enough to listen; you need to act on what you hear. Two sets of issues arise: ○ The first, concerned with children's behaviour and relationships, comes back into the circle to be dealt with by the children themselves. ○ The second involves issues such as 'no water at lunchtime', 'being pushed out of queues' – i.e. school management issues. These need to be discussed in a staff meeting or a school council meeting and a response must be brought back to the children.		
Have I suggested the introduction of a school council to explore management issues? Two representatives from each class take issues raised in Circle Time to a half-termly school council meeting. This also includes representatives from staff, lunchtime supervisors and governors. Any decisions reached by the council are reported back by the representatives at a subsequent circle meeting. The council is also held in a circle and follows the usual structures.		
Do I draw attention to the Golden Rules displayed in the classroom and relate them to the activities in Circle Time? All of the games and activities included in this book and *Quality Circle Time* have been selected to promote the moral values supported by the Golden Rules.		
Do I use the Class Team Honours certificates to celebrate the childrens' success? Children are nominated during Circle Time for this award during the 'celebration' stage. If the majority agree with the nomination the child receives a certificate signed by the whole class. (*Photocopiable Materials for use with the Jenny Mosley Circle Time model* – see Resources.)		

Pupils spiritual, moral, social and cultural development

14. **The weekly Circle Time for each class enables pupils of all ages, at their own level, to reflect on aspects of their lives, to discuss moral and social issues and to express with confidence their understanding of right and wrong and their sense of justice. Pupils learn to listen to others, to be tolerant of other viewpoints and to respect fellow pupils.**

Ofsted

OFSTED inspection, February 1995
Canberra Primary School

QUALITY GOLDEN RULES

	Yes	No
Do the Golden Rules in your school properly reflect the moral values you want to promote? For example ours are: ◉ Do be gentle, don't hurt anybody. ◉ Do be kind and helpful, don't hurt people's feelings. ◉ Do be honest, don't cover up the truth. ◉ Do work hard, don't waste time. ◉ Do look after property, don't waste or damage things. ◉ Do listen to people, don't interrupt.		
Are the Golden Rules separated from the safety routines operating in your school? Safety routines include such points as: ◉ no running in the corridor, ◉ put scissors away, ◉ keep to the right when walking down the stairs. To sum up, the Golden Rules should be displayed in every area of a school. Next to them, in each dining hall/ corridor/classroom etc., a unique set of safety routines specific to that area is displayed.		
Are the Golden Rules golden – i.e. big, bold and gold coloured? Could I put up photographs of children practising the Golden Rules next to the appropriate Golden Rules? (i.e. picture of children being kind, gentle, listening well to each other)		
Have I negotiated, through Circle Time, the details of the classroom safety routines? (e.g. where to put the scissors away)		

	Yes	No
Do I frequently reinforce the Golden Rules through my use of language? (e.g. by saying 'Well done for being kind' or 'Do you know which Golden Rule you are breaking now?')		
Are the Golden Rules actively taught and reinforced in Circle Time meetings through discussion activities, role play etc.?		

Do the words in my incentives system echo the imperatives of the Golden Rules? Do the stickers and certificates say the following things?
 	
   ○   **Well done for being gentle.**
   ○   **I have listened well.**
   ○ **Thank you for being honest.**		

Do I actively model the Golden Rules and teach by example? Am I kind and gentle, do I listen well and do I respect the children's property?		
Do all the children fully understand the philosophy behind the Golden Rules in the school?		
Are the parents given two copies of the Golden Rules to approve: a glossy one to put up at home and a second one to sign and return to the school? On the copy of the Golden Rules to be returned there is a line at the bottom that says I have read and understood the school rules – signed ………… (name of parent).		

	Yes	No
Could I propose a whole-school assembly at the beginning of each term, to which all members of the school community and parents are invited, to focus on the Golden Rules and the safety routines? Many children come from homes which have different Golden Rules from school. One recurring Golden Rule from home seems to be, 'If anyone hits you, hit them back.' For many children there is therefore a culture clash. It is vital after every holiday period to start the new term with an assembly on the Golden Rules.		

Attitudes, behaviour and personal development

37. Pupils are well behaved and courteous and aware that the school has high expectations of them. Pupils respond well to the 'Golden Rules' which provide clear guidance for purposeful and positive relationships with peers and adults. Clear definitions of appropriate behaviour and procedures enable pupils to take responsibilities for their own actions.

 **OFSTED Inspection, July 1996**
Phoenix Secondary and Primary School

5 Quality Golden Time

The core system of Quality Circle Time is Golden Time. Golden Time is the key concept that unites the incentives and sanctions systems in this particular model. It comprises the two sides of the same golden coin. It is precisely this unity that makes the model effective.

The two key features of the model are, firstly, that all 'middle-plodder' children are recognised and rewarded and, secondly, that children are deterred from inappropriate behaviour because they are highly motivated by the incentives.

Unlike other systems, this model has the underlying philosophy of trusting a child from the outset. Children are not required to earn privileges, they are given them by right on a Monday morning. The implicit assumption is that they are trusted and expected to enjoy these. They have a choice to behave well or to break the Golden Rules. If they choose to do the latter, they must accept the consequences of their actions. In this way the system is helping to build the child's inner locus of control (Rotter 1966). Stourfield First School were delighted with the results:

We just have to let you know – not only do we now have Golden Time 'up and running' but we even have a Golden Room!

We have transformed a room with £500 of new activities of the children's choice, with golden stars, golden material, golden blinds and even golden confetti adorns the carpet. It's brilliant. We have 'Good News' slips which go home, and deducting minutes of Golden Time has made our discipline policy simple, but so much more effective – no Corridor Club – no hours spent in reprimand. The staff love it – the children love it and the parents love it.

I thought we had a reasonably positive atmosphere, but Golden Time has shot status and self-esteem right to the roof-beams.

Yours sincerely

Mrs C Kirkham
Headteacher of Stourfield First School

The appraisal and development of Golden Time is linked with Circle Time to support the child in eventually developing self-discipline.

If you are working with nursery or reception children, see p.52 for guidance on the use of Golden Time with younger pupils.

References: see Appendix 2.

THE INCENTIVES AND SANCTIONS SYSTEM

	Yes	No
Did I set up and talk through Golden Time during our weekly Circle Time meeting?		
Did I ask the children to brainstorm all the choices for Golden Time?		
Did I allow all children to enjoy the first Golden Time as a 'freebie', free of sanctions? This provides an opportunity for you to take photographs of the children enjoying the activities – this 'visual cue' can be a great motivator if a child is wavering on the brink of misbehaviour.		
Have I displayed a large Golden Time activities choice list using photographs to illustrate each activity, which each child can then sign up for on Mondays?		
Do I use a whispered verbal warning, then a visual warning system, if a child breaks a Golden Rule? Do I have large laminated warning cards ready to put beside them quietly when they break their Golden Rule?		
Do I remember to remove the visual warning symbols at breaks, lunchtime and the end of day?		
Do I operate the losing five minutes' Golden Time sanction if a child does not respond to a visual warning, and do I record this properly?		
Do I organise all the children who have lost Golden Time to sit quietly around a table with a sand-timer during Golden Time, until their time lost is completed?		

	Yes	No
At the end of each term do I present all the children who have not lost any Golden Time with a Golden Certificate containing the Golden Rules to take home? This also acts as a reminder to parents.		

OTHER CRITICAL INCENTIVES

	Yes	No
Do I ensure that I keep a record of all class team honours certificates awarded to children by children, and signed by children, and make sure that every child is nominated by creating opportunities for others to be calm, helpful etc. and then praising their efforts?		
Do I carefully phrase nominations for class team honours to include all children throughout the term? For example, someone who is always calm/kind.		
If the children make an inappropriate nomination which is not supported by the class, do I have a system to address this? For example, a picture of an attainment ladder which the child can 'climb' to reach their target and achieve the nomination.		
Parents. Do I let them know the system I use?		

> Self-Esteem Builders, LDA's range of motivational materials, was designed specifically to support the Quality Circle Time model. Certificates, stickers, badges, Golden Rules posters and class target sheets are all excellent resources to support your incentives and sanctions system.

GOLDEN RULES

Do be gentle	Do not hurt
Do be kind and helpful	Do not hurt people's feeli
Do work hard	Do not waste other people'
Do look after property	Do not waste damage thin

Keep Golden Rules – gain Golden Time.

Activity	Computer	Extra Art
Week		
Week		
Week		
Week		

Golden Time Activity List – sign up early.

YOUR CHOICE

Break any Golden Rule and you will lose 5 minutes of Golden Time.

Keep the Golden Rules and we will all enjoy each others company in Golden Time.

Loss of Golden Time Chart

ame	5 mins	10 mins	15 mins	20 mins	25 mins	30 m
Carl	/	/				
Amy	/					
Ravi	/					
Binta	/	/				
Ben	/		/	/		

Earning back Golden Time Contract

I agree to ....
.... (target)

in order to earn back .... minutes
of Golden Time.

Keep the
Golden Rules

Signed .... pupil
Signed .... teacher

Teachers decide if they want to give Earning Back Contract.

Five minutes to reflect.

Send the good news home once a term.

A & B Huggett
22 Comfort Drive

Golden Time
Certificate
congratulations .....
you have kept
the Golden Rules

6 A Quality Lunchtime Policy

A child's view of and attitude towards school is shaped by their experiences during the **whole** day. Unhappy lunchtimes can colour or stain this daily school experience and the subsequent unhappiness can prevent the child from fully realising their academic and social potential. If a child has no friends, they quickly learn that they are unlikeable. If a child gains negative attention (which is better than none) through fighting, they quickly learn to become a louder and more violent fighter.

Even your middle plodders are vulnerable. Bad experiences at lunchtimes will 'pull the plug' on the self-esteem building you have worked on all morning. It is, therefore, vital that you give lunchtimes serious consideration. Some teachers are unwilling to move into this area, claiming that it's not their duty. It's not, but if you want to release excellence in your class you will have to encourage them to become involved in this. I have summed up the key issues. There is an expanded section in *Turn Your School Round* (Mosley 1993).

References: see Appendix 2.

A QUALITY LUNCHTIME POLICY

	Yes	No
Could I suggest some ideas during staff meetings to improve the status of lunchtime supervisors? For example, by including them on staff display boards, inviting them to assemblies, including their contributions in newsletters, school brochures etc.		
Could the lunchtime supervisors in my school be given the opportunity to discuss concerns with the teaching staff through regular short circle meetings?		
Do our lunchtime supervisors have good communication with the teaching staff?		
Could the teachers agree to teach playground games as part of our PE policy? Once each half-term you could go out in the playground with your class to play games.		
Are the Golden Rules and safety routines prominently displayed side by side in the dining hall and playground?		
Are the lunchtime supervisors invited to whole-school INSET behaviour days etc.?		
Could the lunchtime supervisors be included in staff social occasions?		
Could my class's lunchtime supervisor be invited to attend some class Circle Times?		
Do the lunchtime supervisors receive copies of the school's newsletter?		
Could I have a two-way post-box for letters from children to their lunchtime supervisor and her replies to them? The post-box could have a photo of the 'dinner lady' on it.		

	Yes	No
Could my class write thank-you letters to send to their lunchtime supervisor?		
Could I suggest to the lunchtime supervisors that they operate a community task force for persistently disruptive children? This would involve a difficult child, along with some responsible volunteer children, being provided with useful work to occupy them. Examples of tasks are helping the caretaker and making items for school use under the supervision of a lunchtime supervisor or volunteer parent. In this way the difficult child is not only kept busy, but learns good social skills and is celebrated for helping the community; so self-esteem is built as well.		
Could I regularly check and update my wet playtime box to keep it novel and interesting?		
Could I instigate 'Tell a Good Tale' after lunch and then invite my lunchtime supervisor to pop in, even if it's just to stand by the door and volunteer a piece of good news about my class? 'Tell a Good Tale' is a brief circle ritual in which children volunteer good news, e.g. someone being kind or helpful to another.		

Letter from Bankwood Primary School.

Our progress is slow and it is taking a lot of time, but we are **very** pleased with what we've done. Circle Time, Golden Time, better lunchtimes and involvement of lunchtimes supervisors are established – playtimes and lunchtimes are much better.

7 Helping children 'beyond'

There are some children 'beyond' all the earlier ideas, even beyond Golden Time. They are the ones who push you beyond your goodwill, beyond your temper limits and beyond your fund of creative ideas of what to do next. However, you can only earn your right to claim this situation has arisen when you can place your hand on your heart and say that you have truly tried and tried again with all the ideas suggested so far.

Remember, these children have not only tested you to your utmost limits, but they have, in the past, tested everyone. Wherever they go, no one's eyes light up with joy to see them. Their mum wishes her child hadn't come back so early; the neighbours wish he hadn't come round; other children wish he hadn't joined their groups; and the teacher wishes he hadn't made it in to school.

Any study of self-esteem theory reveals how significant this series of responses are. The child's self-image or, as C. H. Cooley calls it, 'the looking glass self', reflects only negative pictures from others. If this situation continues, the child only has one option – ie, to become forever the difficult person they see infront of them. (See *Turn Your School Round* for diagrams of the vicious cycles.) It is vital to find ways to give these children back a sense of self-worth, a sense of control over their behaviour and actions by providing a positive image in a guaranteed success policy such as **Tiny Achievable Tickable Targets** (TATTs). The initial stage can be two or three 3-minute sessions in the morning during which the child's target is an agreed standard of work or behaviour which is achievable. Once the child succeeds at that standard, it can be raised or the time period can be made longer. Throughout this period the child's self-esteem can be enhanced by inviting them to attend a smaller therapeutic circle, no more than 10–12 children, all of whom share a range of emotional needs. Here, two adults act as co-workers, in order to guarantee them one oasis a week where they receive unconditional warmth and respect.

It's important to remember that it suits classes to have 'naughty' children in them. The other children know, as soon as they subtly wind up that child, he'll respond loudly and turn you into a whirling dervish yet again. You will then fail to notice that they haven't done the work either or that you are providing entertainment because other children have become bored. A child's behaviour is embedded in a group dynamic. An excellent strategy is to consider making the child's daily target, ie sitting calmly in the seat – the class target. You could use LDA's *Class Target Wall Charts* – or you could easily make your own. The procedure is that you agree, in Circle Time, with the prior permission of the troubled child, that you will enlist the classes support. The child's target can become a whole class target. You display an attractive target sheet poster with the target clearly written at the top e.g. We are all trying to sit calmly in our seats. You explain that every time this child reaches his target he can contribute a reuseable star or fish (re LDA's design) to cover its white outline on the poster. He will contribute the majority of the stars. However, you'd like them to show that they can also 'model' this good behaviour too (*Social Learning Theory*; Bandura). Therefore, during the day, you try and notice the required 'sitting' behaviour of any of the children and then celebrate their success by inviting them to put a star on the poster. Once the poster picture is complete the whole class is given a social treat e.g., parachute time. In this way, the class learn that there is something to be gained from helping this child to be 'good' ie staying on task, as opposed to the previous occasions when there was much to be gained from helping him to be 'naughty'!

References: see Appendix 2.

HELPING CHILDREN 'BEYOND'

	Yes	No
Could I always remember to smile and welcome my child 'beyond' every day, thereby helping us both to start each day afresh? If he doesn't get positive attention straightaway, he'll soon move to 'wrestling' negative attention from you.		
Could I operate a TATTs system, perhaps with a peer mentor, to acknowledge and reward the child's effort? A TATT system ensures his day contains moments of success. Agree a small target for his work or behaviour and let him choose another child as 'mentor'. This child will supervise the target periods and ensure a star/sticker/dot is put into the right square on his special card.		
Could I help this child through Circle Time? As suggested previously, it is a great idea to enlist peer support (see *Effective IEPs Through Circle Time*, M Goldthorpe). With our special scripts; 'Would it help if you … Or 'Would it help if I …?'; it is possible to draw upon other children's goodwill and ability to structure a special action plan to help this child.		
Could I negotiate with the child regarding one unacceptable behaviour which I personally find hard to tolerate? Some behaviours get right under our skin. This behaviour can take away our ability to be fair or calm. It is therfore a good idea to ask a colleague if they would be kind enough to have a table prepared in their room with work on it. You then need to talk to the child and explain that you will give a visual warning if this particular behaviour occurs; if he chooses to repeat the behaviour, it is better for both of you, if he has 'time-out' in the next classroom. There should be a sand-timer put beside his work in that classroom so that he can see how long he has to last.		

	Yes	No
Could I organise a small therapeutic circle for the children 'beyond'? A weekly therapeutic small circle is normally taken by a teacher and one other co-worker. It's vital to have two people so when you think 'I can't be positive any longer, he's driving me mad' the other co-worker takes over being warm and positive! In this way you can guarantee the child unconditional positive regard – essential if you wish to enhance their self-esteem. There should be no more than 10 or 12 children in this group – and it's vital that there is a mixture of children. If they are all 'acting out' they will just role model each others behaviours. You need to invite children with good social skills who may need some extra support during a difficult time in their life. Also, withdrawn children need this sort of support.		
Could I suggest the school operates a task force at lunchtime? Many of our children beyond cannot cope with the wide open unstructured space of a playground. Because they have low self-esteem, they have no awareness of self. They become addicted to being shouted at or hit as it gives them, temporarily, a sense of 'self'. So it is vital, to give them a positive experience at lunchtime. Many schools have set up a task force where children are supervised to tackle tasks which will help the school. In one school, they have a Furniture Renovation group who sand down chairs and drawers, varnish them, and then sell them on at car boot sales, bringing money in to buy playground activities.		
Do I know and 'protect' my crumple button? Each of us, the minute we say "don't fidget … don't mutter" reveal to our pupils our crumple button; what it is that a child has to push to ensure that we turn into an irritable nag. Children beyond are skilled at detecting it. Try not to give it away with a series of "don't do's …". Instead focus on the children that are modelling good behaviour you like and use lots of "Well done for … keeping the chair leg still … staying in your chair … ".		

8 Containment

You may come to a very serious stage. This is when, as a staff, you all agree that the consistent application of the previous strategies has failed and that a particular troubled and troubling child can no longer benefit from the mainstream provision your school is offering. At this stage the emphasis must swing from trying to support the child to saving your sanity and/or the sanity of your colleagues. The headteacher will also need support during the arduous process of completing endless forms and lobbying the authorities to place the child into special education or to obtain special support for them.

CONTAINMENT

	Yes	No
Could I suggest we have a regular Circle Time for staff where these kinds of issues are raised?		
Am I brave enough to ask for help myself and admit that a child is seriously threatening both mine and my class's mental health?		
Could I suggest or accept, if it is for myself, a timetable of support created by the staff? In our culture we are not taught to ask for help and rarely do so more than once or twice. This would involve all members of staff offering an hour or so each day to occupy a child so that you could have a break in order to recover the vision of what teaching can truly be like. It's vital that the other pupils in the class enjoy a time when all tension is lifted from the room. Verbal support is not sufficient. A timetable can really help you pace yourself psychologically.		
Would I be prepared to occupy a troubled child in my class to give a colleague some respite?		
Can I accept that it is not my colleague, my school or myself that has failed this child? It is this particular mainstream system that is failing the troubled child. They need more limited boundaries and contacts to make life and work safer for them. Can I let go of any guilt I may feel concerning this child?		
Am I prepared during this stressful period to step up my personal care plan in order to replenish my 'wells of energy'. Only if you pamper yourself physically and create fun times can you keep a balanced perspective on life. The troubled child is not the whole of your teaching career. All manner of things pass.		

	Yes	No
Am I able, when under stress, to look after myself properly?		

Letting your parents know about the Whole-School Quality Circle Time model

Mr & Mrs Griffin

Don't forget you must let the parents know about the model. You need to send a newsletter with a paragraph on each heading of the model explaining what you do in your classroom. Invite parents to come to Circle Time. Explain to them that we show our respect by not naming people negatively in the circle. Explain some of the ground rules.

Many schools run workshops – Peterborough Primary School in Hammersmith do this and show a film of their Key Stages 1 and 2 Circle Times so that parents understand its potential.

9 Adapting Golden Time for nursery and reception children

The principle of using Golden Time for the incentive and sanction systems operates effectively with nursery children as well as with those at school. However, for young children Golden Time becomes a shorter, daily event and greater use is made of visual prompts.

How to operate the sanctions system

I advocate the use of a large visual display, as illustrated below.

First stage

A large, yellow sun with a smiley face is constructed. The rays of the sun are yellow clothes pegs, but the reverse side of each peg is painted grey. A child's name is printed on the yellow side of each peg, along with a small photograph cut-out of the child's face. The sun represents Golden Time and all the children who are going to enjoy the privilege.

Second stage

If a child breaks a Golden Rule, they are initially given a verbal warning. If they fail to respond to that warning, their peg is removed from the yellow sun and placed on the combined smiley sun and sad cloud. This stage offers the child a choice: to heed the warning and be reinstated on the first sun to enjoy the privilege of Golden Time, or to be removed to the sad cloud and lose privilege time.

Third stage

If the child continues to break the Golden Rules, their peg is placed on the grey cloud with its grey side facing outwards. Additional grey pegs can be placed next to the first to indicate further loss of privilege time.

Golden Time

At the onset of Golden Time, a large sign is put up to enhance the feeling of privilege. This might read 'We're enjoying Golden Time'. Any child with a grey peg on a cloud must sit away from the activity area. A sand-timer is used to show the child how long they must remain seated before being allowed to join in the activities. They must sit and watch the timer quietly and then they will be invited back.

WE'RE ENJOYING GOLDEN TIME

It is important to ensure that Golden Time is fun and creates a community feeling. All the staff and helpers should be included and the activities should be sufficiently varied to maintain enjoyment and excitement. Loss of Golden Time can only be used as an effective sanction if it really is a privilege to be included in it.

Golden Time activities may include singing, dancing to music, playing party games, drama activities, Simon Says and so on.

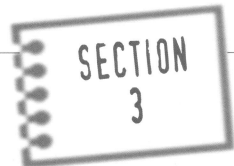

SECTION
3

Building social and learning skills through Circle Time for nursery and reception classes

The skills children need to learn

I believe we try to teach children academic skills too soon! Before learning to read and write they need to know about the skills of looking, listening, speaking, thinking and concentrating.

For nursery children, rather than having whole-class Circle Times, it is better to divide the class into several smaller circles with a maximum number of ten children in each. Each circle can have their own teacher or helper, who each take their circle to a corner of the room at the same time. The children can either sit on chairs or on individual carpet tiles on the floor; carpet tiles create a special space of their own and add to the symbolism of the circle.

Each circle should have its own speaking object, such as a painted papier-mâché egg or a small teddy bear, which a child holds whilst talking. The talking object is passed around the circle from child to child during rounds.

There is a variety of activities designed to use in Circle Times in Section 4. The teacher should select what she thinks is appropriate for a 10-minute circle session. The teacher and helpers should continue to praise children throughout the week for using the skill that has been the focus of the Circle Time. A big picture denoting 'Our Skill This Week Is' should be put up in the classroom.

The teacher needs to hold regular brief Circle Times for the other circle facilitators to ensure that all use the same approach: constant praise, good eye contact, calm voice, use of stickers and so on. If you do decide to divide classes into small circles it is essential to construct the same lesson plan and photocopy it for each facilitator.

The use of stickers during Circle Time to commend the appropriate skills is encouraged; you may need to create opportunities for every child to receive one. If your budget does not stretch to frequent use of stickers, try to be creative about providing tangible encouragement. For example, you could get a stationer to produce a stamp to your own special design – include words and a simple picture. Using this, you could stamp adhesive labels to make your own stickers.

There are special Circle Time stickers on which each skill is symbolised by an animal's qualities; see Self-esteem Builders (LDA). There are the following:

- ◗ cockerel on a microphone – for **speaking** skills
- ◗ owl with cap on – for **thinking** skills
- ◗ eagle's 'eye' – for **looking** skills
- ◗ rabbits with pricked-up ears – for **listening** skills
- ◗ stork with fishing rod – for **concentrating** skills.

You may be able to dream up better ideas!

At the beginning of each session using these stickers, the children point to the special skills they are going to work on.

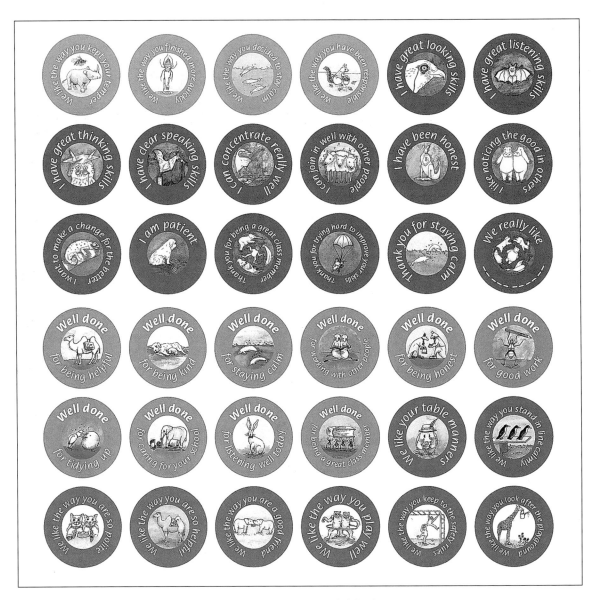

Self-Esteem Builder Stickers available from LDA.

Using rounds to develop learning and social skills

Rounds for looking skills

1. I would like to sit on a cloud because ...
2. What I like best about leaves is ...
3. I like my partner's face because ...
4. I like this game because ...
5. Looking at things helps you ...
6. The photo I liked best was ... because ...
7. In the picture I can remember looking at ...
8. My friend ... [what partner did to change appearance]
9. Sometimes you have to look carefully because ...
10. My favourite object was ... because ...

1. I would like to sit on a cloud because ...

Hold a circle outside to look at clouds. Ask the children to look at their colours, shapes and movement. Do they remind them of anything? Then get them to complete the sentence in turn.

2. What I like best about leaves is ...

Collect boxes of leaves, some green, some autumnal – even leaf skeletons. The children sit in a circle and spread the leaves out on the floor. Then they pick them up and look closely at them. Discuss what they can see (e.g. veins, blemishes, insect eggs, bits eaten). After that, they complete the sentence in turn.

3. I like my partner's face because ...

Get the children to form pairs in a circle. Ask them to look at their partner's hair colour and decide if their hair is straight or curly, long or short. Then they should look at their partner's face to see what colour their eyes are. Ask the children to close their eyes and see if they can picture their partner's face.

Give each child a photocopy of a face with eyes, nose and mouth, but no hair. Ask them to colour in the eyes and hair to match their partner. Finally, they complete the sentence in turn.

4. I like this game because ...

Display ten items. Make up an appropriate story – for example, my nan went on holiday and took ... [name and point to the items, then place them in a box]. Ask the children to think quietly what the items are, then get each child to name one object. As each item is named, take it out of the box and give it to the child who named it to hold.

Alternatively, divide the children into pairs, and give each pair a paper plate with six small items on it. One child closes their eyes and their partner removes two objects. The first child then opens their eyes and says what is gone. They then reverse roles.

The children complete the sentence in turn.

5. Looking at things helps you ...

In the circle, the teacher does some simple actions. The children watch, then copy them. Explain to the children that the actions will be changed without warning, so they need to watch carefully. Alternatively, children may volunteer to lead the actions.

Instead, you could play Follow the Leader. A child chosen to be the detective, closes their eyes. The teacher points to a child, who becomes the leader. The detective then opens her eyes, and moving in a circle tries to discover the leader. The leader must try to change the action when the detective isn't looking. The detective has to guess, by watching the circle of children, who the leader is. Finish with the children completing the sentence in turn.

6. The photo I liked best was ... because ...

Cut out photos of people from magazines and paste them onto card. Show these one at a time to children. Ask what each can tell you about the person from visual clues (e.g. Does the person look sad, happy, angry etc.? Do their clothes give clues about their jobs?) Finish by completing the sentence.

7. In the picture I can remember looking at ...

Find a picture of a lively scene and show it to the children. Ask the children to find things in the picture and then ask questions about them (e.g. What colour is ...? How many ...? What can you see on ...? What is ... doing?). The children complete the sentence in turn.

8. My friend ... [what partner did to change appearance]

First, play Spot the Difference. Make two sets of simple drawings with a slight alteration in one. Ask the children to spot the difference (e.g. the rabbit has only one ear in one picture).

Then divide the children into pairs, and ask them to study their partner's appearance. Explain that, in turn, one child will change their appearance. Give the children some ideas (e.g. roll down one sock, push up one sleeve, take off jumper, turn up collar).

It might be an idea for the teacher to demonstrate by changing her appearance secretly, then asking the children to guess what is different.

One child of each pair turns away while their partner changes their appearance. The first child has to guess what is different. They then reverse roles. Finally, they report what happened by using the sentence.

9. Sometimes you have to look carefully because …

Perform a mime (e.g. taking clothes out of a basket and pegging them on the line). The children have to repeat the mime. Use a set of cards showing various actions to extend the activity. The children pick up a card and act out the mime. The others could guess what it is, or repeat the action. In turn, they complete the sentence.

10. My favourite object was … because …

Bring in a selection of visually interesting objects (e.g. a rock, a shuttlecock, a violin, a cheese grater). Ask the children to look at each object very carefully. In turn they describe one object in detail, using the sentence.

Rounds for listening skills

1. The best thing about this game was …
2. I enjoyed this game because …
3. One thing I heard was …
4. The music made me think of …
5. The person whose voice I guessed the quickest was …
6. One sound I found hard to guess was …
7. I liked this game because …
8. Sometimes you have to listen carefully because …
9. My favourite nursery rhyme is …
10. The thing I like listening to most is …

1. The best thing about this game was …

The teacher claps a rhythm. The children listen, then repeat it. The teacher then claps a different rhythm for them to repeat. In turn, the children use the sentence to say what they liked about the game.

2. I enjoyed this game because …

The teacher says a nonsense phrase (e.g. Iggley Wiggley Tinga Tong) for the children to listen to and repeat. This can be made more complex as children become proficient. Ask them to make up their own nonsense phrase for everyone to repeat. They finish by completing the sentence in turn.

3. One thing I heard was …

An outdoor circle. The children shut their eyes and listen. In turn they say what sounds they have heard.

4. The music made me think of …

Buy or make a tape of different musical excerpts. The children listen to them and say what mood/scene/picture each suggests to them.

5. The person whose voice I guessed the quickest was …

The children sit in an outward-facing circle. The teacher gives them a simple phrase to repeat (e.g. Jack and Jill went up the hill). The teacher says they are to close their eyes and she will gently tap a child on the shoulder. They must then repeat the phrase. Other children have to guess who spoke. This is repeated several times. End by asking the children to complete the sentence in turn.

6. One sound I found hard to guess was ...

Make a tape of familiar sounds (e.g. vacuum cleaner, washing machine, filling a bath with water, shutting a door). Ask the children to listen to and identify each sound. They finish by completing the sentence.

7. I liked this game because ...

You need a metronome for this activity. Set it at different tempos. The children listen to each tempo, and march on the spot in time. Finish with them completing the sentence in turn.

8. Sometimes you have to listen carefully because ...

Play Chinese Whispers. The teacher whispers a sentence to the child next to her, who whispers this to the next child and so on around the circle. The final child says the sentence aloud and it is compared to the original. End with a round to complete the sentence.

9. My favourite nursery rhyme is ...

The teacher says a familiar rhyme, line by line, but changes a word in each line. The children listen carefully and repeat the rhyme exactly as they heard it.

> e.g. One, two polish my shoe,
> Three, floor knock at the door.

Ask a child to try this with a different rhyme. The rest copy them, as before. Then they say in turn what their favourite nursery rhyme is.

10. The thing I like listening to most is ...

The teacher sings different notes in a variety of ways (e.g. high, low, loud, soft, short, long, with mouth open wide or nearly closed). The children copy her. A child could be asked to try leading the activity. The children finish by saying in turn what they like listening to.

Rounds for speaking skills

1. Choice of rounds
2. I like this ... because ...
3. When I am happy I say ...
4. What should I say if ...
5. Tom spoke to me about ...
6. I am going to teach you about ...; this is what you do.
7. Brainstorm ideas
8. When I grow up I want to be ... and I will ...
9. One thing I will take on my picnic is ...
10. My family is special because ...

1. Choice of rounds

e.g.   My favourite dinner is ...

My favourite storybook character is ... because ...

One thing I don't like is ... because...

It's good to have a friend because ...

One thing I like at school is ...

2. I like this ... because ...

The children are asked to bring in a special object from home (preferably not a toy). Examples to give them could be a photograph, a shell collected from the beach, an interesting object (e.g. something of Mummy's or Daddy's, something with an unusual shape). Each child says a sentence about why the object is special or what they particularly like about it. This can be continued over several short circle sessions until all the children have had a go.

3. When I am happy I say ...

The teacher tells the children that the way in which we speak often tells people something about the mood we are in. The teacher gives an example by repeating a sentence, for example 'Come into the kitchen', to reflect different moods (e.g. happily, fearfully, angrily, etc.) and asking the children to guess the mood. The teacher then instructs the children to repeat some sentences, telling them which mood to reflect each time. They finish by completing the sentence.

4. What should I say if ...

The teacher has a puppet, and tells the children that the puppet wants their help in learning to say things correctly. The puppet is then used to ask the children how to say various things. This can be used to teach about correct procedures, manners and so on. Each question begins with 'What should I say if ...'

Suggested topics are:

> I want to use the toilet in lesson time.
>
> I want to join in someone's game.
>
> I have accidentally hurt someone.
>
> I want to use something that someone else is using.
>
> someone is being horrid to me.

The children offer suggestions and agree on the best way to ask. You could finish with a round to complete: 'I am pleased with Perky Puppet because he said ... very nicely.'

5. Tom spoke to me about ...

The children work in pairs. Tell them to ask their partners questions to find out as much about them as possible. You may need to give examples, such as what they like/dislike to eat, what hobbies they have, what pets they have, their favourite toys/TV programmes. Allow a few minutes to prepare for this. Then each child, in turn, states one to three facts (depending on ability) about their partner. They could use the example 'Tom spoke to me about ...' or make a report, such as 'Tom has a dog called Benjy. Tom likes baked beans. His favourite toy is Action Man.'

6. I am going to teach you about ...; this is what you do.

Tell the children they are going to prepare a simple explanation of how to perform a task which they will give in the next circle session (or over several sessions). It is best to go through this with the class and decide which task each child will explain so that the teacher can offer suggestions and stress that the children must pay attention to all the details involved. Examples of possible tasks are: cleaning out the hamster, polishing shoes, getting dressed, wrapping up a present.

7. Brainstorm ideas

This is a less personal activity. The children think about what happens at different times of the year or in different places.

> e.g.   Winter is a time for ...
>
> At the seaside you can ...

8. When I grow up I want to be ... and I will ...

The children talk about what they plan for the future.

9. One thing I will take on my picnic is ...

The children work in pairs to discuss and plan a picnic – what they will take to eat, where they will go, how they will get there and so on. If this is not appropriate, focus on a different type of event. In turn, they suggest an item to complete the sentence.

10. My family is special because ...

Each child completes a sentence about their family. The teacher can spend some time giving the children suggestions about things to say (e.g. number of siblings, something about Mum and Dad, what the family like to do together).

Rounds for thinking skills

1. One thing in my dream bedroom is …
2. One thing on my planet was …
3. The best objects …
4. We could help our planet by …
5. One thing I would like to give to a poor child is …
6. I liked this game because …
7. The hardest thing to guess was …
8. The person I like best is … because …
9. The thing I like best about school is …
10. If I were King/Queen I would …
11. Twenty questions

1. One thing in my dream bedroom is …

Tell the children to close their eyes and think of their dream bedroom. You could use the following to give them ideas:

> How is it decorated? Are the walls papered or painted?
> What colour are they?
> What posters, pictures or designs are on the wall?
> What is your bed like?
> Is it a special shape, like a boat?
> Maybe it's raised and you have to climb a ladder to reach it?
> Think of yourself lying in your dream bed.
> Does it have a special duvet cover and pillow case?
> What do they look like?

Now ask them to decide on some of the really exciting toys they might have in their bedroom. They should think of each one in turn and imagine playing with it. Which is their favourite?

Go round the circle, asking the children to say one thing each to complete the sentence.

2. One thing on my planet was …

Use the following to stimulate ideas:

> Close your eyes. Think of yourself visiting a strange planet. First of all, imagine you are in a spacecraft. What is it like?

> Think of all the gadgets and knobs and levers in the spacecraft. What do you think you might see out of the window? What do you think space would look like?
>
> Imagine you have landed on the planet and are standing outside the spacecraft. What does the planet look like? Does it have trees, grass, flowers, the same as Earth? Is everything there the same colour or different colours from on Earth? Think of the animals on the planet. Are they like cats and dogs, horses and cows, or are they strange looking?
>
> Imagine you see some houses. What shape and colour are they? Do they have doors and windows?
>
> Imagine what sort of creatures or people live on this planet. Do they look like you? Think of trying to talk to them. How could you make them understand you? What would you ask them?

Then the children each say one thing to complete the sentence.

3. The best objects

Ask the children to think of three things that they could put in a box and send to another planet which would tell the inhabitants what children are like on Earth. Brainstorm ideas, then get the children to discuss which are best. Then ask them to vote for each in turn to decide on the best three.

4. We could help our planet by ...

Encourage the children to think of ways in which we could be less wasteful or recycle things at home or at school (e.g. using both sides of drawing paper, not cooking more food than can be eaten). Together, get them to decide on a small project that they would be involved in for a limited time (e.g. recycle one type of household item). Finish by asking them to complete the sentence in turn.

5. One thing I would like to give to a child in a poor country is ...

Ask the children to think of all the things that they have that children in poor countries might not have (e.g. electricity, warmth, shelter, clothes, sufficient and varied diet, medicine, toys, television, outings). Encourage them to decide on something they would like to give to a poor child, and get them to complete the sentence in turn.

6. I liked this game because ...

The teacher collects a selection of mystery objects in a bag (e.g. toothbrush, fork, purse). The children ask questions about each object until they have guessed its identity. The teacher can give clues and help guide the questions until the children are familiar with the game. Finish with a round in which they complete the sentence in turn.

7. The hardest thing to guess was ...

The teacher assembles a collection of gadgets or utensils which are probably unfamiliar to the children (e.g. bicycle tyre lever, paperweight). The children look at each item and think what it might be used for. The teacher can then demonstrate its correct use. At the end, the children each complete the sentence in turn.

8. The person I like best is ... because ...

The teacher collects a selection of pictures of interesting-looking (but not well-known) people from magazines. The children look at each picture in turn and say what they think the person is like and what the person might do for a living. They finish by completing the sentence in turn.

9. The thing I like best about school is ...

Ask the children to give their views on education. (e.g. Why do you think it's important for children to go to school? What do you think would happen if children didn't go to school? What do you think are the best things about being in school? What do you think are the bad things about being in school?) In turn they complete the sentence to say one thing they like about school.

10. If I were King/Queen I would ...

Ask the children to imagine they are the King or Queen. Now encourage them to think of one nice thing they would like to do for all the children living in their country. Get them to complete the sentence in turn.

11. Twenty questions

The teacher, or a child, thinks of a famous person. The children are allowed to ask twenty questions requiring a yes or no answer to try to find out the identity of the person. This can be done with children taking turns to ask questions so that everyone has an opportunity to join in.

Exercises for concentrating skills

1. This was fun because ...
2. Sometimes you have to concentrate really hard because ...
3. Substituting words
4. Walk, Hop and Jump
5. Numbers
6. Simon Says ...
7. Wink Statues
8. Animals
9. Chinese Mimes
10. Word Association

1. This was fun because ...

The teacher chooses a story to read aloud and selects four or five nouns which are frequently repeated throughout the story. The children are instructed to perform particular different movements every time the selected nouns occur in the story (e.g. tap head for one noun; tap shoulder for another; tap knees for a third; stand up, turn round and sit down again for a fourth). They must concentrate on the story in order to perform the actions at the correct time. They finish by completing the sentence in turn.

2. Sometimes you have to concentrate really hard because ...

The teacher chooses a selection of small objects and arranges five or more (depending on the children's digit span memory) in a row. The children study the selection for a few minutes, then close their eyes while the teacher removes one object. The children then open their eyes and say what is missing. If the number of objects is increased, two or more may be removed at a time. Variations to this include substituting different objects and changing the sequence of the objects. Finish by asking them to complete the sentence.

3. Substituting words

The teacher says a list of items (e.g. dog, cat, horse, cow). She then repeats this, substituting one different word (e.g. dog, cat, mouse, cow). The children have to say what the new word is and what it should have been.

4. Walk, Hop and Jump

Get the children to push back the circle of chairs to make a large space inside to move about in. Instruct the children that you will blow on a whistle – once for walk, twice for hop and three times for jump. The children move about the circle as instructed. They must concentrate on not bumping into anyone. If two children 'touch', they must stand still on that spot. Change the movement from time to time by blowing a different number on the whistle. The game ends when most children are stationary.

5. Numbers

Children are numbered 1 to 6 around the circle. The teacher calls a number and gives an instruction (e.g. number 3s swap seats. number 5s stand up and hop three times, numbers 1 and 4 shake hands). The children whose numbers have been called follow the instructions.

6. Simon Says ...

The children stand. They follow instructions from a child or teacher in the centre of the circle, but only when the words 'Simon says' are put before the instruction. For example, if the instruction is 'Simon says put your hands on your head', the children follow this. If it is 'Touch your toes', the children disregard the instruction. Anyone who does not respond correctly is out and sits down.

7. Wink Statues

The children sit in an inward-facing circle. A detective is chosen and leaves the room. A wizard is then chosen. The detective returns and stands in the centre of the circle. The wizard then winks at a chosen child, trying to do so unobserved by the detective (e.g. winking when the detective's back is turned). The child must "freeze" until the end of the game. The game continues with more "victims" until the detective identifies the wizard.

8. Animals

The teacher thinks of a four-word sequence (e.g. cat, dog, horse, cow). The children in turn say 'cat, dog, horse, cow' around the circle. If a child says an incorrect word, the next child begins the sequence again. When the sequence has gone around the circle twice, the teacher can introduce a new one.

9. Chinese Mimes

The children stand sideways in a circle, their right shoulders pointing to the centre, their eyes closed. The teacher taps child A (the child in front of her) on the back. Child A opens her eyes and turns to face the teacher, who mimes an action. Child A turns to B (in front of her) and taps him on the shoulder. Child B opens his eyes and turns to face Child A, who repeats the teacher's mime. This continues around the circle. Once the children have completed the mime they keep their eyes open. When the mime reaches the teacher, she repeats the original mime to the class to show how much it has changed.

10. Word Association

The children play Word Association around the circle with two claps in between; for example, tree, clap, clap, leaf, clap, clap, flower, clap, clap, yellow, clap, clap, sun and so on. If anyone is stuck for a word and the rhythm is broken, they begin with a new word.

SECTION
4

Developing creativity within Quality Circle Time

Circle Time must grow, change and develop

All the instructions about Circle Time sessions that I have previously offered (in *Turn Your School Round* and *Quality Circle Time*, Mosley 1993, 1996) have been very prescriptive. They have incorporated 'fail-safe' sessions with firm structures and ground rules. By working through their lesson plans, hopefully you will have built up both your and the children's confidence. It is now time – still keeping to the same ground rules – to extend yours and the children's creativity, spontaneity and imagination. The children should by now associate Circle Time with emotional safety and respect; therefore Circle Time becomes the ideal space in which to encourage new and exciting responses.

The activities in this section suggest the use of various props, all of which can be bought as the *Quality Circle Time Kit* from LDA.

11 Activities using puppets

As early as 1908, Jacob Moreno concluded that Viennese children were acting out the problems of their daily lives during their play (Moreno 1934). His observations and work eventually led to the introduction of many brilliant active groupwork approaches within education. Melanie Klein (1929), writing on play therapy, noted that children were able to express their inner feelings through play with puppets and dolls and that these objects could personify significant figures in their lives.

Despite that early pioneering work, the use of puppets is still a neglected teaching resource for young children. I have therefore decided to draw further attention to this very valuable strategy.

Children have the ability to suspend disbelief with puppets so that the characters become very real and their interactions become meaningful. Children are therefore very willing to enter into a dialogue with the characters and profer wonderful advice or ideas totally spontaneously.

The value of these conversations with the puppets lies in the children's realisation that they can be agents of change; that they possess the power within themselves to find solutions to problems and then to put these solutions into effect.

This empowerment builds up their 'inner locus of control' (Rotter, 1966) as children see that events can be controlled by their own capabilities. Using puppets is also an effective way of exploring morality in a clearly demonstrable way as children closely involved with the 'characters' easily see the moral values involved. They then determine the moral outcomes.

I was impressed once again by the power of puppets very recently when I was working with a circle of 9–14-year-olds in a special school in Essex. These children had very varied learning, behavioural and emotional needs. During the hour-long circle session I introduced a variety of games and drama activities and the puppets. At the end, the children were asked what they had liked the best and most responded with 'The puppets ...' because they 'made friends with each other'.

In the following staff Circle Time, the teachers said how moved they had been, especially when the children asked if they might stroke or kiss the puppets goodbye. Many of the children had difficult, fragmented and painful lives and the staff felt that the children had been empowered by the role they had been given in helping the puppets achieve a happy ending. In Gestalt therapy, (Perls, 1969) this would be termed achieving 'closure'. Even if it was for only a brief moment, the experience gave the children an insight into how happiness could be created.

The following sketches are based around the moral values embodied in the Golden Rules. When you feel more confident and are not intimidated at the idea of putting fluffy animals on your arms and accompanying your hand movements with a series of strange voices, then you can start improvising sketches for yourself based on children's suggestions.

The puppets are called Salt and Pepper in the sketches. Teachers can substitute suitable names suggested by the children for each new sketch.

References: see Appendix 2.

Theme: sharing

Salt I went to Pepper's house yesterday to play. We had a really good time. I played with all her toys and she even let me have a go with her new [put in something topical]. She's going to come to my house today to play with me. Oh, I think she's here now.

Pepper Hello, Salt, I've been so excited about coming to your house to play with you. We had such fun yesterday. What are you playing with?

Salt It's a new castle and soldiers my mum and dad bought me.

Pepper Can I play with it too? We could make up a story together.

Salt Oh, I don't think so. It's new and I haven't played with it much myself yet. You can play with something else.

Pepper All right. I know! I'll build a house with the Lego bricks.

Salt You can't do that. I've made a rocket out of them and I don't want it taken apart.

Pepper Hmm, what shall I do then? I could colour in a picture in this colouring book.

Salt I don't want you to use my pencils! You might break them.

Pepper takes out a packet of sweets.

Salt What have you got there?

Pepper Mum bought me some sweets. Would you like to share them?

Salt Yes, please.

Pepper counts ten sweets.

Pepper There are ten, so we can have five each.

Pepper counts out five sweets and hands them to Salt.

Pepper Now what shall I play with? I'll play with the space station and astronauts.

Salt   I was just going to play with them myself. I'm going to make an intergalactic battle between the astronauts and the soldiers.

Pepper   Well, can I do a jigsaw puzzle then?

Salt   I don't think you'd better. You might lose a bit.

Pepper turns to the children.

Pepper   This isn't much fun. Salt won't let me play with anything. I think I'll go home.

Pepper turns to Salt.

Pepper   I have to go now, Salt. I'll see you another day. Goodbye.

Salt talks to the children.

Salt   Well, Pepper didn't stay very long. I think she's mean to go so soon. I stayed all afternoon at her house. Don't you think she's mean?

The children can explain to Salt that he is at fault for not sharing his toys with Pepper.

Salt   Oh dear, I can see now that I'm the one that is being mean. Pepper let me play with her toys and shared her sweets with me but I didn't share with her. I didn't think about her feelings at all. What can I do?

The children offer suggestions.

Salt   I will say sorry to Pepper and promise that if she will come and play at my house again, I will share my toys with her.

Development

Children can devise a list of sharing ideas for the classroom and the playground. For example, 'share our game' could be used to help integrate shy or isolated children into a playground game. This may initially need some adult supervision, especially if the child is isolated because of unsociable behaviour.

Theme: friendship – being helpful

Salt talks to the children.

Salt   I'm going to call on my friend Pepper to see if she wants to come to the park with me and take turns with my new skateboard. Hello, Pepper. Would you like to come to the park and play with my new skateboard?

Pepper   That would be really nice, but I have to do some jobs first to help Mum..

Salt   How long will you be?

Pepper   Well, I have to wash up, tidy the kitchen and polish the furniture in the lounge. I think it will take about an hour to do these jobs and then I can come to the park with you.

Salt   Hmm, I don't really want to wait that long. Never mind, perhaps you could come another day. Goodbye then.

Salt moves away from Pepper, then stops and turns to the children.

Salt   It doesn't seem a very friendly thing to do, leaving Pepper at home with her jobs while I go to the park and have fun. I am her *best* friend. What do you think I should have done?

The children offer suggestions.

Salt   Pepper, if I help you with your jobs we can finish them in half the time and then go to the park.

Pepper   Thank you, Salt, you are such a good friend.

Development

The children could have a round of 'I was helpful when ...'. See also *Quality Circle Time* (Mosley 1996), Section 13, Key Stage 1, circle meetings 11, 12 and 19.

Theme: friendship – make friends, break friends

Salt and Pepper are playing together with a toy farm. Salt picks up a tractor which is on the ground near Pepper.

Pepper Hey, give me back that tractor! I had it first.

Salt Well, you'd finished with it and I need it for the farmer to pull the hay trailer.

Pepper I hadn't finished with it. I was going to use it again. Give it back.

Salt No, why should I? I want it.

Pepper tries to snatch the tractor from Salt. They have a tug of war with it.

Pepper Let go. I want the tractor.

Salt No, you let go. I want it!

Pepper I'm having it.

Salt No, you're not! I'm having it.

They continue to pull and tug at the tractor. Suddenly Salt lets go.

Salt Right, have the silly old tractor. I'm not going to play with you ever again.

Pepper I don't care. I hate you and I don't want you to play with me anyway.

Salt and Pepper move apart.

Teacher Goodness me, what was all that arguing about, Salt and Pepper? I thought you were friends.

Salt It's Pepper's fault. She took my tractor.

Pepper No, it's not. It's Salt's fault. He wasn't playing with it until I wanted it.

Salt It's her fault.

Pepper   It's his fault.

Teacher   Dear me, this isn't the way in which friends should behave.

The teacher addresses the children.

Teacher   Salt and Pepper are both sad now. They really like each other but they have had a quarrel and are not friends. Does this ever happen to you? What do you think they should do now?

The children offer suggestions.

Teacher   Right, Salt and Pepper, you have heard all the ideas that the children have suggested. What do you think about each other now?

Pepper   I don't really hate Salt. He just made me angry, that's why I said it. I would really be sad if we weren't friends any more.

Salt   I would be sad too. Sometimes people quarrel about things that are silly. The tractor wasn't really important to Pepper or to me, not like being friends – that's really important.

Teacher   Now that you know that being friends is more special than having the tractor, how you going to make friends again?

Pepper   I'm sorry that I quarrelled with you, Salt. I do really like you and I want us to be friends again.

Salt   I'm sorry too, and I do want to play with you again.

Pepper   I know, you have the tractor first so that the farmer can collect the hay and then I'll have it to take the cows to market.

Salt   Thank you, children, for helping us to see how silly we were and how important friends are.

Development

The teacher displays a chart with two columns. These could have different-coloured columns. The children are asked to suggest 'kind' and 'unkind' words to write in the appropriate column. Children could brainstorm all the good qualities of friendship and why it is important for people to have friends.

Theme: name calling

Teacher tells children that Salt has a surname which is Mellie and this sometimes causes problems for him.

Pepper talks to the children about Salt.

Pepper Look, children, there's Salt Mellie. We call him Smelly Mellie. (chants) Smelly Mellie, Smelly Mellie. Come on, children, you join in with me if you want. It's really good fun. Smelly Mellie, Smelly Mellie.

Salt moves away and puts his hands over his eyes.

Pepper Where's Smelly Mellie gone?

Pepper looks around and then moves over to Salt.

Pepper There you are. What's the matter? Why are you crying?

Salt You don't know what it's like to be called a horrid name. It makes me really sad inside.

Pepper But it's only a name. It can't hurt you like a stick or a stone.

Salt Yes it can. It can hurt. Children, tell her how it can hurt. Talk to the children about it, Pepper, and ask them what they think.

Pepper Is this true, children? Can horrid names hurt your feelings and upset you? Can you tell me how they make you feel?

Pepper listens to the children.

Pepper Thank you for telling me this. I didn't mean to hurt Salt, I was just having a bit of fun. I didn't know that it would upset him. I'll go and talk to him.

Pepper moves over to Salt.

Pepper Salt, I've listened to what the children had to say. I realise now that it was unkind of me to call you a horrid name and

I'm sorry that I hurt your feelings. I promise that I will not call you that name again.

Development

Have a round of 'My name means'. Each child states their name and gives it their own unique pretend meaning. (e.g. My name is Darren, which means 'fast runner'. My name is Leila, which means 'kind and helpful'.)

Theme: feeling left out

Pepper is sad and dejected.

Teacher   Pepper, you are looking very sad. What's the matter?

Pepper   I haven't got anyone to play with.

Teacher   Why don't you ask some of the other children if you can join in their game?

Pepper   I'm too shy. They might say no, and then I'll feel even more miserable.

The teacher addresses the children.

Teacher   Poor Pepper. She feels very lonely and left out. Do you think it sometimes happens at school that some children don't have anyone to play with and feel left out?

The teacher must make sure at this stage that no actual child is named.

Teacher   How do you think you would feel if you had no one to play with and saw all the other children having fun together? What do you think we could do to stop people feeling lonely and left out?

The children discuss practical ways of dealing with this problem, perhaps by creating 'playground friends' (i.e. a few children volunteer to take on this role and actively seek out and play with children who are normally not included in others' games.

The teacher calls Salt.

Teacher   Salt, Pepper is feeling very lonely and left out because she has no one to play with. Do you think you could be kind and ask her to join in your game at playtime?

Salt   Poor Pepper. I was too busy playing and having fun to notice that she didn't have anyone to play with. Yes, I'll go and ask her now.

Salt goes over to Pepper.

Salt   Would you like to join in a game with me and my friends at playtime? We'll show you what to do and explain everything to you.

Pepper   Thank you, Salt. I would like that very much.

Development

The children form small groups and take turns to role play the lonely child asking to join in a game the others are playing (e.g. Ring-a-ring o' Roses). Perhaps teachers or lunchtime supervisors could teach the children some playground games which would involve a number of children; see *Quality Circle Time* (Mosley 1996) for other ideas.

Theme: a special person

A mirror inside a box is needed for this session. It should be small enough to be easily passed around a circle of children.

Pepper	Hello, Salt. You don't look very happy today. Is anything wrong?
Salt	I'm fed up because I'm not really good at anything. Danny is really good at running and Parvi is good at reading, Rachel can do all her maths and James is the best at football. Everyone seems to be good at something except for me. I feel so ordinary and a nobody.
Pepper	Well, Salt, I've got a box here and if you look inside you will see someone who is really special. Would you like to have a look?
Salt	I suppose so.
Pepper	But you must keep quiet and not say who the special person is yet.

Salt looks in the box and says 'Oh!' in surprise.

Pepper	Children, would you like to look in my box and see who the special person is? You must keep very quiet and not say anything until everyone has had a look.

The children pass the box around the circle and look at the reflection of themselves in the mirror.

Pepper	Now, children, you have all had a look at the special person inside my box. Who was it?

Pause.

Pepper	Yes, it was you. All of you are special. I'm special and, Salt, you are special.
Salt	But how can I be special when I am not good at anything?
Pepper	Everyone is good at something, Salt. You are good at being

kind and helpful. You're good at looking after your pet hamster and you're good at telling jokes.

Salt   Yes, I suppose I am. I didn't think about those things. They didn't seem important.

Pepper   Everything we are good at is important to someone or in some way.

Salt   I feel so much better now, Pepper. I don't feel I'm not important any more.

Salt turns to the children.

Salt   Let's all say together, 'I am special'.

The children repeat this several times.

Development

The children complete a round of 'I am good at ...'. It is important to stress that they may choose something at school or at home so that everyone can find some skill to celebrate. Make sure that no derogatory comments are made in response to any child's statement.

Theme: bullying

Salt and Pepper are in the playground. Pepper has chosen a site to use as a home base. This could be something specific to your individual playground, perhaps an area or a piece of equipment the children are familiar with.

Salt   You can go and play somewhere else, Pepper. My friends and I want to use this for our den.

Pepper   But we were here first and this is our home in our game.

Salt   I don't care, I want it now.

Salt starts to push Pepper and continues in a loud voice.

Salt   Go on, get out, go away!

Pepper addresses the children.

Pepper   Salt is always like that. He has a very bad temper and if he doesn't get his own way he pushes or punches or kicks the other animals. Lots of us don't want to play with him any more because he is a bully. If he doesn't change soon, he won't have any friends left. Could one of you tell him for me?

One child could volunteer to call Salt and tell him that he must stop being a bully and hurting others, or no one will like him.

Salt   I just can't seem to help it. I get very angry and then it happens and I push or punch someone. I don't really mean to be horrid and I don't want everyone to hate me, but I don't know how to stop it happening. Can you think of any ideas that might help me?

With the teacher's guidance, the children offer suggestions. These might include an incentive for every week that Salt avoids becoming involved in bullying. Salt might suggest a sanction that he thinks would be effective. The children can discuss how the whole class could become involved in Salt's behavioural target, with a special treat (e.g. a session of parachute games, an outing, a disco) if they succeed in helping Salt to change.

Salt   Thank you, children, for your suggestions. If you remind me and help me to be better I think that I could change and stop hurting others.

Development

An Open Forum could be held for any child who needs help to stop bullying. Children could write out, or the teacher could photocopy, the Golden Rule:

Do be gentle. Don't hurt anybody.

The children can illustrate these and make a wall display of their work.

Theme: Salt's bad day

Salt addresses the children.

Salt   I'm having such a bad day. Everything is going wrong. This morning when I got up I tripped over a book and fell over. I cut my knee on a model plane and broke the plane as well and it was my best one. Then there were no Frosties left for my breakfast and I had to have yukkie toast, the postman didn't bring my special offer football stickers and I really, really wanted them to come today. Dad had a flat tyre on the way to school so I was late and [teacher's name] was cross because I left my reading book at home. At playtime my best friend Dean went off with someone else and I was on my own and felt miserable. I couldn't do my numbers today, I just kept getting them wrong. Mum made me the worst packed lunch in the world, my head hurts and I'm fed up.

Teacher   Oh dear, Salt, you are having a bad day! We all have bad days, don't we, children, when everything seems to go wrong for us? What do we need on bad days to help us feel better?

The children make suggestions (e.g. something nice to happen, someone to be kind, something to cheer us up).

Teacher   Can you think of any good ideas that might cheer Salt up?

The children offer suggestions (e.g. someone inviting Salt to join in a game, telling Salt good things about himself, Salt asking his mum to make his favourite tea).

Salt   Thank you for your ideas. They have been really helpful. I feel better already just thinking about them. Perhaps you could think up ideas to help each other when someone is having a bad day, and you could be especially kind because having a bad day is really horrid and you need people to understand and care.

Development

The children could develop cheering-up ideas to use in the classroom, such as making an 'I'm having a bad day' badge; the other children must try to be especially kind and considerate to the wearer.

Theme: don't waste time

Salt and Pepper have been given some work to do by the teacher. Salt is busy working while Pepper is looking around.

Pepper   Hey, Salt, I've got a really good joke. Do you want to hear it?

Salt   Not now, Pepper, I'm busy. I want to finish my work.

Pepper looks round again.

Pepper   I think I'll tidy up my pencil-case.

Pepper makes tidying movements.

Pepper   There, that's better! I'll try them out now.

Pepper makes drawing movements.

Pepper   Hmm, that's really good. Salt, look at this funny face I've drawn.

Salt   Shh, do your work.

Pepper   I will in a minute. Oh look! My hands are dirty from the pencils. Please, [teacher's name], can I go and wash my hands?

Teacher   Yes, be quick.

Pepper moves along a little way.

Pepper   I'll just have a peep in the window of Mr Bishop's class and see if I can see my friend Jo. Oh yes, there she is! (*Starts waving.*) Oh no, Mr Bishop's seen me! I"d better go.

Pepper moves along a bit more.

Pepper   Oh, there's a nice display of pictures. That's Samir's – he's done a really good rabbit – and who did that house? Oh, Donna. I don't think Amy's is very good, it's a bit messy. Gosh, Jake's done a brilliant space monster. Oh well, I'd better go and wash my hands.

Pepper moves off, washes hands and then moves back.

Teacher   You've been a long time, Pepper.

Pepper   Sorry, [teacher's name], I needed the toilet.

Teacher   Well, hurry up now and get on with your work.

Pepper   Now, what shall I write about? Oh, look out of the window! I can see a cat climbing up the tree. I think it's trying to catch a bird. Up it goes, higher and higher … now it's crawling really slowly along the branch … hurrah, the bird has flown away! … I wonder if the cat will be able to get down.

Teacher   Right, children, you can stop working now. Salt, what did you write about looking after pets?

Salt   I wrote about getting a book from the library to learn what to do and making sure you give the right food and have the right sort of place for your pet to live in. Some pets might need to be exercised or brushed every day.

Teacher   That's very good, Salt. Now, Pepper, what have you written about different types of holidays?

Pepper   Um, well, I haven't actually written anything yet.

Teacher   But, Pepper, what have you been doing?

Pepper   I sharpened my pencils and tidied my pencil-case, then I needed the toilet and then the lesson had finished.

Teacher   It seems, Pepper, as if you have wasted time instead of getting on with your work. You will have to stay in after lunch and do it then.

Pepper   Oh, but [teacher's name], I've brought my new skipping rope to school to play with.

Teacher   Well, Pepper, you have to finish your work first. I hope that you will remember not to waste time again.

Development

The children could brainstorm all the reasons why they shouldn't waste time. Suggest that they think of a class motto to encourage them to work, and then write it up and illustrate it. The children could make their own sand-timers.

Theme: keeping the rules

Salt and Pepper are in the playground.

Salt   There are some really big apples on the tree behind the caretaker's shed. Let's go and climb it and get some apples to eat.

Pepper   But you know we are not allowed to go there and we are not supposed to climb trees either. It's the school rules.

Salt   I don't care. They are silly rules and I'm not going to keep them. Come on, let's get some apples. No one will see us.

Pepper   I'm not going to.

Salt   You're just a scaredy cat. Cowardy, cowardy, custard.

Pepper   I'm not scared and I'm not a coward. It's stupid to break the rules and get into trouble. You're the silly one. Rules are made to keep us safe, they take care of us and the school. If there weren't any rules people would always be getting hurt and belongings and property would get damaged.

Salt   Well, you can keep the rules if you want to. I'm not going to. I'll do just what I want to do.

Pepper   That's not the right way to think. Rules are made to help us all but everyone must help others by keeping the rules. It's called being responsible. Why don't you ask the children what they think?

Salt   All right then.

Salt turns to the children.

Salt   Do you think I should go behind the caretaker's shed and climb the apple tree? Why not?

The children suggest reasons.

Salt   I'm beginning to see what rules are there for. If everyone was like me and broke the rules we wouldn't be safe, nor would our belongings and property be safe. We have to be –

what's the word? – responsible for everybody's sake. Thank you, children, for helping me to understand about rules. I can see now why it is silly to break rules.

Development

The children could suggest other useful rules for their classroom and playground and discuss why they are important. They could also think of ways to help everyone keep the rules.

References: see Appendix 2.

12 Activities using a cloak

In this chapter some ways of using a cloak in a Circle Time context are suggested.

One of the effects of wearing a costume and taking on a role is that it removes the restrictions and limitations of everyday life.

Children become free to explore situations and experiences beyond their normal range. Taking on a role may offer status to those children who normally do not enjoy it. Moreover, role play within the circle creates a safe environment in which to act out and explore contentious issues. The teacher can introduce an appropriate costume to create a specific role and, therefore, specific situations to role play and explore. When taking on a role, children often have the courage to say things which they would not dare to say in real life.

Wizard or Wizadora Wonderful

Think carefully which child would benefit from having this real boost of self-esteem.

When a child wears the cloak, they become Wizard Wonderful. They can wish for something pleasant for the whole class (e.g. the child might say 'I wish everyone will go to the seaside' or 'I wish that everyone gets what they really want for Christmas'). Some of the wishes could be acted out (e.g. the children could mime being on a beach looking for shells, building sand castles, splashing in the sea). Another suggestion is that each child mimes opening a Christmas present in turn, and then using it so everyone has to guess what it is.

Older children could be encouraged to wish for more sophisticated things (e.g. 'I wish that no one ever quarrelled again' or 'I wish nobody was ever ill'). The other children thank Wizard Wonderful for their kind wish and, if appropriate, discuss the outcomes of the wish granted (i.e. how they would use the wish or what benefits they would enjoy).

Star turn

The child chosen to put on the cloak becomes a famous person (past or present) of their choice. They may either give clues by speaking or by mime (perhaps holding up cards made by a helper with appropriate text). They tell the other children why they have made their particular choice (i.e. what they like about this person or what this person does). The children sit in a circle and ask questions – the child in the cloak doesn't have to be factually accurate in their replies.

The children may need some time to think about their choice, and should be encouraged to be imaginative and not just choose the latest pop star or football hero. The teacher could make suggestions to children with limited experience, based on attributes they admire (e.g. someone strong could be King Arthur).

This activity could be turned into a small project to research a character of their choice. Children who find acting difficult will need help in order that their presentation is as competent as other children's.

Someone special

Each child can have a turn at wearing the cloak once a year and becoming the focus of positive attention. Younger children might like to wear a special hat or crown as well as the cloak. The child sits on a chair in the middle of the circle and the other children offer positive comments about them. (e.g. Sarah, you are kind. Sarah, I like the colour of your hair; it's really golden. Sarah, I like the way you smile a lot. Sarah, I think you are really good at drawing faces.)

The teacher needs to be aware that some children will elicit far more positive comments than others. It might be a good idea to focus on certain children's positive qualities in front of the other children during the few days prior to their turn.

Children will need to be reminded that only positive comments are allowed and that these do not include ones like 'Danny, I like the way that you frighten the younger children' or 'Leena, I like it when you are rude to Mrs Davis.' The children can also ask questions. (e.g. 'What's your favourite food?', 'What pop star do you like best?') For those children who cannot think of a question, you could have some prepared cards with a different question on each for them to read.

My special place

When a child puts on the cloak they can wish to be anywhere of their choice, either real or imaginary. They describe the place to the other children, saying why it is so special and what they like to do there.

Encourage the children to be as imaginative as possible – anything is allowed in their special place. When the child puts the cloak on, the children could all put on an imaginary cloak. They could draw or paint the cloak or tell the next person about it. The other children close their eyes and try to visualise the place. If appropriate, they could offer their own positive comments and additions.

Performer of kind deeds

Each child in turn puts on the cloak to make the statement of intent that they will do something kind for someone else. This can be used as an 'encourager' when a specific act of kindness is required (e.g. a child is lonely and needs to be included in another child's game) or more generally when considering kindness.

The object of the intention could be someone out of school. (e.g. 'I will help Mummy clear up after tea.') Encourage the children to translate their intentions into actions, perhaps reporting the outcome afterwards.

Follow the Wizard or Wizadora!

The cloak can be used for a variety of games based on the 'Simon Says' format (see page 72). Wizadora may perform actions for the other children to copy or give commands (e.g. walk like a giant, scamper like a mouse, eat like an elephant – prepared beforehand!). If necessary, prepare some cards in advance to give the children ideas.

The Wizard's or Wizadora's kitchen

For this activity the teacher will need to cut out about forty food items from magazines and paste them onto cards. Since this is quite a time-consuming task, older children could perhaps do this instead.

The wizard stands in the middle of the circle. The cards displaying the items of food are spread out on the floor halfway between the wizard and the seated children.

The children are alternately named **Elf** or **Goblin** around the circle. On the teacher's command, all the elves enter the circle and try to collect the scattered food items. Any child touched by the wizard returns to their seat empty handed. The goblins then have a turn. This continues until all the food items have been removed or for a set number of turns.

The child who has collected the most food items (or one who is specifically chosen) becomes the new wizard. The cards are scattered on the floor and the game is repeated.

Wizard or Wizadora's spell book

Wizadora is blindfolded and sits on a chair in the centre of the circle. A book is placed under her chair to represent her book of spells. Children take turns to creep across the circle and try to capture the spell book.

If Wizadora hears the child approaching, she shouts 'Stop!' and points in the direction of the sound with her wand. If she is correct, the child returns to their seat. If not, the child can continue to try to reach the book. The child who successfully captures the spell book becomes the new Wizadora.

Making spells

One child is chosen to be the wizard and another to be his apprentice. The wizard has to think of a good spell (e.g. the sun will shine, all sick animals will become well, babies will sleep through the night) – ask them for ideas.

Children volunteer appropriate ingredients for the chosen spell. They need to be encouraged to think of different things for each. (For the sun to shine, these could be yellow sunflowers, burning coals, oranges; to cheer someone up, ingredients could be a joke book, a cuddly toy, a card.)

When a child volunteers an ingredient, the apprentice mimes collecting it and takes it to the wizard, who puts it into his golden bowl (a waste-paper bin will do).

When all the ingredients have been added, the wizard stirs them together with a wand. The children could devise a chant to say together while this is happening.

The wizard then mimes performing an appropriate action with the magic spell (e.g. throwing it into the air, sprinkling it over the other children). All the children 'suspend disbelief' and cheer as if the event wished for were really occurring.

At the end of each spell the children give the wizard a clap.

Transformation

Any child wearing the magic cloak can transform themselves into an animal of their choice. The child mimes being the animal and the other children try to guess what it is. Once they've guessed, they slip off their chairs and become that animal. When all the children have become that animal, the child wearing the cloak waves a wand and they all return to their seats.

13 Activities using rounds

Rounds are an important feature of Circle Time because they include all the children and encourage even the shy and withdrawn child to participate in completing a simple sentence stem. They can be used for many different purposes: to build self-confidence, to enhance self-esteem, to encourage team-building, to elicit fears or worries and to celebrate success.

A 'talking object' such as a decorated wooden egg or a small teddy can be used during a round. Each child, in turn, holds the object and completes the sentence stem. The importance of this is that no child may be interrupted while they are holding the talking object, which encourages those children who at other times might be swamped by the more exuberant members of the class.

It is a wonderful moment when a shy/chaotic/autistic child holds the egg. Any child who does not wish to participate can say 'pass', but those children who do elect not to speak must be given another opportunity to take their turn at the end of the round. It is important not to rush those children who need more time to collect their thoughts. Otherwise they might feel intimidated and choose to 'pass' as the safer option. Some may twist it through their fingers or even rock meditatively; and all children wait, patiently offering eye contact. It's a magic moment as it shows real respect for the different ways in which children think. If we, as teachers, always take the first answer, we are giving the message that the brashest and fastest are the best! It is vital that we 'role model' that taking your time is fine and respecting that fact is something we believe in. Rounds embody this philosophy. Sometimes it is a good idea to prepare children by telling them the subject of the round in advance so that they have more time to consider their contributions.

It is useful to have a suggestion box into which children can place their own ideas for future rounds. Some ideas are given here.

1. I'm happy today because …
2. I like/don't like being out in the playground because …
3. I like/don't like celebration assembly/Golden Time/Circle Time because …
4. I found sums/writing/reading difficult when …
5. I would like to be … [name animal, flower, tree etc.] because …
6. Behind my magic door would be …
7. I feel pleased/sad/angry/frightened/excited when …
8. My special wish is …
9. Wouldn't it be wonderful if …
10. The best surprise I would have is …

14 Activities using a treasure chest

Like all props, the treasure chest acts as a stimulus for creativity and encourages children to use their imagination. The children themselves may think of different ideas for using the treasure chest. Having become accustomed to using a prop, the teacher may feel more confident about introducing other items. Chairs are an example; with some creativity and imagination they can become all manner of things. In rows they become buses or trains; draped with a cloth, a chair can become a throne; upturned they can be obstacles. The more children can be encouraged to use their creativity through this type of approach, the more they will be able to use it in their academic and social contacts.

Treasures

The children can take turns to bring in a 'treasure' which they place in the chest. They need to be shown the chest first to see what size their treasure must be. It can be any small object that holds a special memory for them (e.g. a shell that they collected from a beach while on holiday, a photograph, a dried flower from a bridesmaid's bouquet, a letter). During Circle Time the children each remove their object from the chest and explain to the other children why it is precious and what it means to them.

A wishing necklace

Some beads (enough for each child in the circle to have one) are placed in the treasure chest. The teacher prepares a length of string, sufficient to make a necklace. Each child in turn takes a bead from the chest and makes a silent wish as they thread it onto the string. The resulting necklace could become a 'cheering-up' item which any child could wear when feeling sad. The other children would make a special effort to be kind and cheer up the wearer.

Treasure stories

The treasure chest is filled with odd items of jewellery which the children and teacher supply (e.g. rings, brooches, earrings, cuff links, bracelets). The children take turns to choose an item from the box and make up a story about whom it belonged to and where they found it. Any child who finds this activity difficult can ask for suggestions from the other children. For special needs children, use card costumes and cut-out people. The children put the jewellery on correctly. This may be developed by each child putting on an item and being the person who featured in their story, by using a different voice and talking for a little while about their chosen character.

Special photographs

Each child brings in a photograph of themselves. They are all placed in the treasure chest. The children take turns to remove a photograph and describe who it is (using no names) to the other children. Remind the children of the ground rules: only positive comments are permitted. The other children have to guess who is in the photograph.

Objects of interest

The teacher places in the treasure chest a few items of interest which may be related to topics the children have studied. The teacher takes one of the items from the chest and asks for a volunteer to become a TV reporter and talk to the others about it. This can be repeated several times with different items and the activity can be done on several occasions.

Daily treasures

You could have an ongoing activity, 'What's in my treasure chest today?' Each day a different object is placed in the box and the children are asked, 'Who would this object be special to and why?' For example, a whistle could be special to a referee, a lifeguard at the swimming pool, a British Rail guard or a policeman. You could develop this by helping the children to invent a story about the 'adventure' this object has endured. This is done as a story round, personifying the object and encouraging them to use fantasy (e.g. Using a 20p piece, the first child starts: 'Well, the day I came out of the factory I felt all shiny and clean and then …'.

Objects could include such things as a penknife, a microphone, a toy stethoscope and even basic things like a jar of water – which would be very special to someone lost in a desert or travelling in a drought-ridden country. Try to include objects which will make the children think beyond their own circumstances and environment.

My special treasure

The teacher talks to the children about treasure being whatever we place value on. They think about what sorts of things we might value in life because they bring happiness, pleasure or satisfaction. The children should be prompted to think about such things as friendship, belonging to a family, health, freedom, peace, the satisfaction of succeeding at something and making a special effort.

Each child is asked to write down one of these treasures on a piece of paper and they are all placed in the treasure chest. The teacher and children then take a treasure out in turn and read it to the class.

Some children may find this activity difficult. They could either write out their treasures at home with help, or work in pairs so that a more able child can help and encourage them.

The golden coins

The treasure chest can also be used to enhance self-esteem. For example, the teacher could place golden coins inside, with each child's name written on one. As a coin is taken out, the other children volunteer positive statements about the named child as they receive the coin. (e.g. 'You deserve the golden coin because you are so calm/thank people/smile/came into school on time.')

Special awards

The treasure chest could contain stick-on stars or jewels. At the end of each Circle Time several children could be selected to award one of these to someone they think has been especially kind or tried hard during that week. The teacher would need to keep a record of who had been selected in order to allow each child to be included.

The treasure keeper

The treasure chest can be used as a prop in games or drama activities. In Keeper of the Treasure, the chest – containing something noisy such as a bunch of keys – is guarded by a blindfolded child. Another child is chosen to try and creep up on the keeper and steal the treasure without being heard. If the keeper hears and successfully identifies the position of the would-be thief by pointing in their direction, another child is chosen to try and capture the treasure. The child who succeeds becomes the new keeper and the game is repeated.

A treasure chest story

The children could make up a story around the treasure chest as a class venture. They subsequently act this out and perhaps perform it to another class.

15 Activities using a rainstick

The following ideas for use with the rainstick can be seen as an introduction to ways of stimulating the children's imaginations. An alternative noise-maker could be used (e.g. wind effects, rattles, drums). Having completed the activities here, children could be encouraged to devise their own creative dramas incorporating the various sound effects.

It is a good idea to teach the children some basic relaxation techniques before starting these activities. For many children, silence is a strange phenomenon which they need to become accustomed to. The children should practise breathing slowly and rhythmically to help them to become relaxed. They can sit on a chair or lie on the floor. If you have been doing parachute work, one idea is to get them to lie down underneath the parachute, as if they are under a blanket together. The children lie in a circle, their feet inwards. They close their eyes and practise breathing from their stomachs: in through their noses to the count of 3, then exhaling through their mouths to the count of 3. They could place their left hands on their stomachs and their right hands on their chests to feel the movements of their bodies as they perform the breathing exercise.

Before each activity with the rainstick, prepare the children so that they are sitting or lying comfortably, breathing rhythmically, and are relaxed with their eyes closed.

The creative visualisations with the rainstick are intended to encourage the children to use their imaginations, in particular with regard to the five senses.

On a beach

You are walking on a beach which is made up of tiny pebbles. You can hear the pebbles scrunching under your feet with each step you take [shake rainstick to make appropriate sound]. Can you feel the tiny pebbles between your toes? Imagine what they feel like ...

It is warm and sunny. Think of the sun on your face ... imagine its warmth.

Now think of it on your back, feel the heat as you walk along ... You can see the blue sea, twinkling and glittering in the sunlight ... imagine that you are walking down the beach to the water's edge [shake the rainstick to simulate walking on the pebbles].

You decide to lie down on the pebbles, feel yourself sinking into them, imagine them trickling through your fingers ...

You are near to the sea now. You can feel the breeze from it gently wafting over your body. Can you taste the salt in the air?

You can hear the waves are rolling in and then the wave trickles back out again [tip the rainstick slowly to make this sound]. Breathe in and out to the rhythm of the waves.

Waves in – inhale slowly through your nose. Waves out – exhale slowly through your mouth [repeat several times].

Quite far away you can hear the waves crash onto some rocks [tip the rainstick quickly to make a louder noise].

You feel warm and relaxed. Think of a gentle thought that makes you feel warm inside, like stroking the cat, cuddling someone you love, watching a happy television programme ...

The beach scene is going to fade away gradually but no one can take away your special gentle thought. Tuck that special thought into your memory box. You can get it out in your mind if you ever need to cheer yourself up. And now I want you to open you eyes and smile at as many people as possible.

An Amazon rain forest

It is perhaps worth prefacing this guided image with basic information about a rain forest so that the children have some idea of what to imagine. If you have any available, show them some pictures or slides or a television programme.

You are standing in a rain forest. The trees are very tall. Imagine tilting your head back to try and see to the very tops of the trees. It's a long way up ...

There are lots of big leaves on the plants around you, much bigger than the leaves on trees in this country. Think about these big green leaves – some of them are so big you can stand under them ...

It is raining [use rainstick]. *Hear the rain drumming down onto the leaves. Think of the raindrops bouncing off a big leaf ...*

Now feel the rain on you. It is not cold rain but warm, and it feels like – a warm shower. The raindrops are big and splash onto your face and run down your back. You can taste the warm rain on your tongue ...

Around you, you can hear the noises of the rain forest – birds and animals. Imagine brightly coloured parrots screeching. Think of their different colours ...

Now you hear chattering noise. It is monkeys. They are swinging from branch to branch at the top of the trees. Listen to their chattering, watch them scampering along the branches and leaping from one tree to the next. See how they sail through the air between the branches ...

Imagine that you are a monkey at the top of the tall, tall tree. Hear the rain drumming on the leaves [use rainstick]. *Think of yourself scampering along a branch ...*

Now you leap off ...

Feel yourself flying through the air like a bird ... then landing on another branch.

You feel happy, you are having fun. Keep this nice feeling with you when you leave the rain forest behind.

Warm at home

Imagine you are in a nice house. It could be your home or a make-believe house. You look out of the window. It is cold outside. There are big black clouds in the sky. You can hear the wind howling and see the trees swaying and the leaves swirling around on the ground ...

It begins to rain [start rainstick gently, then increase so the rain gets harder].

You are glad you are indoors. Imagine how you would feel if you were outside – cold, wet and miserable. Feel a shiver run down your back and feel the cold rain on your face ...

But you are not outside, you are indoors ...

There is a coal fire burning. Feel the lovely warmth from the fire spread through your body, starting with your toes, moving up through your legs, then over your body and down your arms to your fingers ...

See the red and yellow flames dancing on the coals. Watch their different shapes ...

The rain outside is drumming hard on the windows [loud rainstick] *but you are cosy and warm.*

You smell something delicious cooking. What is it?

Imagine your favourite hot food and think of its smell ...

Now imagine you are eating it. Think of the taste and texture and how much you are enjoying it ...

It's raining outside but you don't care because you are indoors and you feel happy and contented.

Keep this nice feeling with you as you come back to the classroom.

A cave by the sea

Imagine that you have found a cave by the sea. You decide to go in and explore it. When you enter, it is very dark.

At first you can't see anything. You feel your way along the side of the cave. The stone is hard and cold. Imagine how it feels under your hands ...

You move very slowly because you don't want to trip over anything.

Move one foot at a time [rhythmic breathing].

Right foot – inhale. Left foot – exhale. [repeat several times]

You can hear rushing water [use rainstick]. *You move towards the sound.*

Your eyes are getting used to the dark by now and you can begin to see things. You see that the rushing water is coming from a stream.

It enters the cave very high up and gushes down the wall. It is very loud now [loud rainstick].

You look at how fast the water is falling. It ends with a big splash in a pool.

You walk further into the cave. Sunlight is shining down into it through a shaft. You can see the cave walls. What do they look like? What can you see?

There is soft sand under your feet. Imagine how it feels, think of it between your toes while you walk ...

You sit down by the pool in the cave. The water gently laps against the sides [tilt the rainstick back and forth slowly to make gentle lapping sounds].

All you can hear is the gentle rhythm of the water. It is so calm and peaceful.

You keep this calm feeling inside you as you come back to the classroom.

Rowing down the river

A parachute is needed for this visualisation as well as the rainstick. The children sit in a circle, feet inwards, and grasp the edge of the parachute in both hands. With a little practice it is possible to synchronise a rowing motion.

You are sitting in a rowing boat on a wide river. You are going to start rowing and listen to the sound your oars make as they splash through the water. [Establish a rhythm of rowing in time with the rainstick. You can also use the breathing exercise; i.e. inhale through the nose, exhale through the mouth with each stroke.]

Now you are rowing well. The boat is gliding through the water. Think of the ripples spreading across the river as you move along ...

What can you see on the river banks and in the meadows beyond? Think of the trees and plants you can see ...

Can you see any animals on the river bank or in the meadows? Imagine what they are doing ...

[If the children are capable of adjusting their speed, the rate of rowing can be changed by shaking the rainstick faster or more slowly.] *You are all pulling well together and your boat is skimming across the water. Imagine the wind on your face as you race along ...*

You trail one hand in the water. It feels cool and soothing as the water gently pulls through your fingers ...

What can you see floating on the surface of the water? Leaves being carried along? Insects skimming the surface? Bubbles breaking on the surface? Perhaps you can see a beautiful blue/green dragonfly ...

You are a good team and you have all worked hard, your arms are beginning to tire and feel heavy. You gradually slow down until you stop ...

Now lie back and relax completely.

A train journey

The rainstick can be shaken to simulate the noise of a train starting slowly, then gradually gathering speed.

> *You are sitting in a train waiting to go on a journey. Feel the excitement as you wait for the train to start moving. Now it's off. Imagine the carriage rocking and lurching as the train pulls away from the station ... listen to the sound as the train slowly gathers speed ... [rainstick]*
>
> *Think of the buildings you are passing. What do they look like? Houses? Shops? Big offices? ...*
>
> *The train is moving out of the town and into the countryside. You are passing farms. What can you see on them? What are the people on the farms doing? What animals can you see?*
>
> *The train is going into a tunnel. It is very dark, you can't see anything. All you can hear is the sound of the train [rainstick].*
>
> *The train is beginning to slow down as it enters a station. Listen to the rhythm of the train as it gets slower and slower ...*
>
> *Think of the train entering the station. Who can you see on the platform? What are they doing? ...*
>
> *The train has come to a stop and your journey is at its end.*

Other ideas

Older children can work in groups and make up their own creative visualisations with the rainstick.

The rainstick could also be used as a signal for children to perform certain activities: in a game, creative dance, a mime and so on.

16 Activities using a blindfold

A blindfold can be used to help children concentrate more effectively on the senses other than sight: touch, hearing, smell and taste. It can also be used to build up trust as the child wearing the blindfold can learn to rely on classmates or a partner for information. The children will probably be quite inventive at thinking up new activities themselves to be done with the blindfold.

Guess who?

One child is blindfolded. The teacher leads the child around the circle to another child. The blindfolded child gently feels the other's face and hair and tries to guess their identity. They then swap roles. Finish with a round of: 'I guessed it was ... because ...'

Guess what?

A child sits on a chair in the centre of the circle, wearing the blindfold. The teacher selects an object from a box and gives it to another child, who takes it to the child in the centre. The blindfolded child feels the object and tries to guess what it is. The children each have a turn to guess an object. Each could finish with a sentence beginning: 'One thing that is harder when you close your eyes is ...'

Squeak, Piggy, Squeak

A child sits on a chair, wearing the blindfold. Another child is chosen to sit on their lap. The child wearing the blindfold says, 'Squeak, piggy, squeak' and the other child responds by squeaking three times. The blindfolded child tries to guess the identity of the 'pig'. After several turns, finish with the round: 'I enjoyed this game because ...'

Tap, Tap

The teacher collects a number of objects (e.g. jam jar, tin, wooden brick, stone) and a metal spoon. A child wears the blindfold. The teacher taps one of the objects with the spoon and the child tries to guess which object has been tapped. Continue until everyone in the circle has had a turn. Finish by completing the sentence: 'One thing that is better when I close my eyes is ...'

Pin the Tail on the Donkey

The blindfold can be used for a game of Pin the Tail on the Donkey, Pin the Chimney on the House and so on. Finish with a round of: 'I pinned the tail/chimney on ...'

Find the Object

A child is blindfolded. The teacher gives another child an object to hold. The children guide the child wearing the blindfold to retrieve the object by saying, 'Freezing, cold, warmer, hot, boiling' as the blindfolded child walks around the circle. Finish with a round of: 'The best thing about this game was ...'

Funny Faces

An activity just for fun is to ask each child to have a go at drawing a face whilst wearing the blindfold. They could finish by completing the sentence: 'My face was funny because ...'

Hunter and Hunted

Two children wear blindfolds and stand inside the circle. One is the hunter and the other the hunted. The hunter has to rely on listening for movement to locate and catch the hunted. The other children must be very quiet and gently guide the children in blindfolds with their hands away from the edge of the circle. When the hunter has captured the hunted, two other children are chosen for the roles. To finish, all the children close their eyes and have a round of: 'When I close my eyes I can picture …'

Obstacle Course

The children build an obstacle course inside the circle. One child wears the blindfold and the other children take it in turns to give directions to guide the child wearing the blindfold around the obstacles (e.g. 'Two steps forward', 'One step to the right'). Finish with the round: 'I had to listen carefully because …'

Take it in Turns

The children work in pairs. One child is blindfolded, the other gently leads them round obstacles. The roles are then reversed. When everyone has had a turn, do a round of: 'I had to lead my partner carefully because …'

17 Creative visualisations

Most of today's children are used to high levels of noise, but also, within their heads, have a whole cacophony of sound. Our culture has become faster and louder. Yet what I and many hundreds of teachers have discovered is that children, like adults, long for stillness and tranquillity.

The creative visualisations offered here are calm journeys during which children can clear their minds and focus on the exciting world of their own imagination. What children are learning is that they, rather than a television or video, have the power to create other worlds. Not only do they learn to have confidence in and enjoy their imaginations, but they also learn that they can make choices in their stories. They have the inner power to shape outcomes. When you withdraw from others and rely on your own inner resources, you are on the first stage of a path moving towards drawing on a higher spiritual self.

Initially, it is vital to teach the children some breathing exercises. Some children – due to their mistrust of life – daren't even close their eyes. Do persist.

Sometimes I do a visualisation after parachute work so that children can lie on the parachute, heads together, feet pointing outwards. Sometimes I do one sitting on chairs in the circle, and sometimes I do one outside Circle Time.

If the tension in the classroom is intense, the children can be asked to sit at their tables with their heads resting on their arms. The simplest breathing exercise is to ask them to close their eyes and imagine that their shoulders are sloping down so that all their worries slip off and away.

The children should be told to breathe deeply from their stomachs, not just their chests. They should inhale slowly through their noses to a count of 3 and exhale slowly through their mouths to a count of 3.

You, also, need to relax before reading out the visualisation. It is highly recommended that when you have finished the visualisation you use the following script to help the children leave the story behind and re enter the class.

"Children, I am now taking the story away. I can't take away your wonderful imaginations and the ability you have to make brilliant pictures in your minds whenever you want to. But now we let go of the story by taking a deep breath and when you breathe out, blow the story away.

You are now very pleased to be back with all the familiar friends in your class team. See how many eyes you can smile into by the time I quietly count to 5. And now I would like you all to smile into my eyes and then we can go on to our next activity.'

Some of the following passages feature on the cassette tape which is available as part of the *Quality Circle Time Kit*, available from LDA.

On another planet

You are going to imagine that you are a space traveller visiting a planet in a different solar system.

At the moment you are in your spacecraft speeding through space. You can feel the padded, lightweight suit transform you into a much larger, puffed up shape. What can you see around you as you look out of the window? Think of the colours and shapes that you can see ...

You are arriving at your destination. You make all the right preparations and step out of your spacecraft into a strange world. Think of how it looks. What are these trees and flowers like? They are very different from the ones on Earth. Imagine the colours and the shapes. You cannot resist feeling the trees. They are so unusual. What are they like to touch? ...

As you look around you and you look up you notice birds in the trees, but these are not like any birds you have ever seen before. What do these birds look like? ... Are they making any noises? What type of noise is it? ... Then you can see animals moving around on the ground. What are they like? They look friendly enough but they are extraordinarily different from any animal that you've ever seen before. What colour and shape are they? ... You can't resist, you stop to stroke one of the animals. Imagine how that animal feels under your hand ...

You walk on a little further on this strange planet until you reach some houses. Do they look like your house or are they very different? In your thoughts describe the way these houses look. How would you explain them to someone back home? ...

You can't resist, you want to find out who lives in the houses, so you call out, 'Is there anyone there?'

The door is opened by a strange, gentle figure. Imagine what this figure looks like. The figure looks friendly, but does it look like you, or anyone you know, or is this figure completely different? ... This figure talks to you. What sort of sounds does it make? Can you understand it? Think about how you are able to have a conversation with it ... You enter the home, the figure has welcomed you in and you look around you. What can you see? Think of all the details of this unusual and imaginative home. How are you going to describe it to people back on Earth? ...

This figure or creature or whatever you want to call it has offered you something to eat and drink. Imagine this strange food. It's very unusual. Think of its smell and the taste. Do you like those textures? Is it nice on your tongue? ... Do you have to chew it very much? Are you enjoying it? ...

You thank the creature for its hospitality and walk back to your spacecraft. As you leave the strange planet, you think of the memories you will take away with you and what you will tell your friends back on Earth ...

I wonder whether they will believe you? And if not, I wonder if you could draw them some pictures that will convince them?

The helping genie

Imagine that you are a genie whose special job is to help others. One day you are sitting in your garden in the warm sunshine watching the small white fluffy clouds float across the blue sky. You are feeling relaxed and contented as you listen to the birds singing in the trees.

Suddenly, you hear your name being called and you see three children in your garden. They are looking very sad, so you ask them what is the matter.

The children tell you they come from a nearby village. They tell you that a giant who lives in a castle at the top of a mountain visits their village each day to steal the vegetables from their gardens and food from the shops, so they are now very hungry.

You agree to help the children and decide that you will visit the giant's castle to see what you can do.

It's a long way to the castle. The road is steep and winding. Think of yourself trudging slowly up this road. You feel your legs getting heavier with each step you take. You are walking slower and slower. You feel very tired …

But you are a genie with magical powers, so you decide to turn yourself into something else to make the journey easier. It might be a bird to soar up into the sky and glide effortlessly on the wind or it might be a fast, four-legged animal. What are you going to choose to be? …

You have reached the castle gates. They are so big they seem to stretch right up to the clouds. Just look at how tall they are – you feel as small as a mouse …

You are now going to go back to your normal self, your little genie self as you creep through the gates and into the castle.

Imagine how quietly you are tip-toeing. You do not want the giant to hear you … You can see the giant's table and chair. How big are they compared to you? …

You have some giant steps to climb. How are you going to do this? Think of how you can manage to get up those steps ...

You now enter a huge room. It is piled high with all the food the giant has taken from the village. Imagine this mountain of food, filling the room! What can you see in it? Loaves of bread, shiny red apples, tins of baked beans, huge packets of cereals? Think of as many different types of food as you can ...

Suddenly you hear a loud thumping noise. The floor shakes and the walls vibrate to the sound. The giant is approaching ...

You do not want the giant to see you. You need to disguise yourself. What can you turn yourself into so that the giant won't notice you? ...

The giant clumps into the room with a bag full of food. What does he look like? Can you see him in your imagination? Can you see how big he is? Can you see what he is wearing? Can you see exactly what he looks like?

The giant sits down in his chair and suddenly, to your surprise begins to cry great big, salty tears that run down his nose and plop onto the floor with a loud splash.

Now, you are a helping genie and you don't like to see anybody unhappy, even giants. You decide you will speak to him and find out what is wrong.

How are you going to approach him? What would you say to the giant? ...

The giant tells you that he is lonely and has no friends. You know that the villagers would be friendly to the giant if he was kind to them and stopped stealing their food. What could you say to the giant as you explain this to him? ...

The giant agrees to return all the food to the village and to be kind in the future and to think of others.

Well done! And now imagine you are the giant. What kind things can you think of that you would do for the villagers? What happy, special treats and acts could you possibly imagine would make people happy. Think of all those things now.

A special day with a friend

Imagine that you are going on an outing to somewhere really special and exciting with a friend. Think of where you would most like to go and what you would most like to do in all this world ...

Now imagine that you and your friend are ready to leave. Picture the two of you very clearly. What are you both wearing? How are you looking? Are you smiling? ...

Feel the excitement and anticipation as you are waiting to set off. Feel the happiness of being with your friend and think of all the reasons why you like this friend so much ...

You can travel to your destination any way that you wish – in a horse and carriage, a posh car, a rocket, a boat. How will you choose to travel?

Imagine the journey in your chosen form of transport ...

You have now reached your destination. Where is it? What does it look like? Picture it clearly in your thoughts ...

What will you and your friend do first? Imagine every detail of what you are doing and think of the pleasure and enjoyment you would feel ... [long pause]

It is now time for lunch. You can choose anything you like to eat. Think of what this meal would consist of. Imagine all the different tastes and the textures and the delicious smells of the food. How marvellous it would be ...

Now imagine the nice, full feeling that you get after you have eaten a great meal and you feel strong enough and ready to get back to your special day out. Plan very carefully in your mind how would you spend the rest of the day? What would you and your friend do? Imagine all the ways you could have some fun and how happy you would both feel ... [long pause]

Keep that happy feeling inside you as you travel back in any way you wish right back to your home ...

Favourite things

Today you are going to think about and enjoy the memories of favourite things in your life.

First of all, I want you to imagine yourself in your favourite clothes. What do you look like? Have you got a very clear picture of yourself? ... Why do you like these clothes so much? Do they feel nice to wear?

Now think of your favourite meal. What does it smell like? ... Think of yourself eating this meal and try to remember the taste ...

What is your favourite television programme? Imagine that you are sitting down watching it now ...

If you were a character in this programme, who would you be? Think of yourself on television as this character and what you would be doing ...

Now you are going to think of your favourite toy. Picture this toy and think of why you like it best ... What do you do with this toy? Imagine yourself playing with it.

Think of your favourite activity outside school. Imagine yourself doing this ... Why do you like it so much? How does it make you feel? ...

Think of your favourite person. What do you do with this person? ... What is so special about this person that makes you like them best? ...

Finally, think of your favourite place. Where do you most enjoy being? What do you do there and why is it so nice?

Special presents

Everyone likes to give and receive presents, so today you are going to imagine what sort of presents you would give if you could choose anything in the world.

First of all, think of your mum and what she would like better than anything else. Imagine her unwrapping this special present. Think of what she would do and say ...

Now picture your dad or brother or sister and imagine the present you would give them. Think of what they would do when they had taken the wrapping paper off and found such a wonderful present ... Now think how pleased and happy they would be ...

Now picture your best friend. What present would you really like to give to them? How do you think that they would react? ...

Think of your school. What do you think would be the best present to give to your school that all the children could enjoy? Imagine the children in the school using this present ...

What would you like to give to children who are ill in hospital that might give them pleasure and happiness? Imagine taking this present to the hospital and all the children there being excited and pleased with your gift ...

Now think of poor children in another country who do not have nice homes, plenty of food or lots of toys to play with. Think of one present that might make them happy ...

You have all been so kind and generous with your gifts that you can now give yourself a really special present. Imagine what it would be and how you would feel to have it ...

An amazing adventure

You have been asked by the King of Westerly to travel to the land of High Ridge and bring back a large and precious diamond from a cave at the foot of Mount Snowcap. It is a long, difficult journey and a fierce dragon guards the entrance to the cave. But you are allowed to take three friends with you to help you retrieve the diamond.

Imagine the three friends you choose to go with you? ...

You must pack your rucksacks before you set off. What useful things will you take with you? A rope, a torch, food, drink, warm clothing? Picture all the different things that you will put into your bags that you might need on this long journey ...

You now set off. Imagine walking together on a wide path through meadows. You come to a large river. Think of the water glistening in the sunlight. It is very wide and there is no bridge. How are you going to get across to the other side? Do you have anything useful in your rucksacks or can you and your friends make something? Imagine the plans you are going to make so that you are able to cross the river ...

You travel on further. Feel the weight of your rucksacks on your back and the heaviness in your legs. You are feeling very weary ...

You stop for a rest. Imagine the relief as you put your rucksack down. Feel your arms and legs relaxing. Breathe deeply and relax ...

Now you are going to eat. What food did you remember to bring with you? Think about taking it out of your bags and sharing a meal together ...

Someone has remembered some lovely refreshing drink. What do you choose to drink?

It is time to set off again. You have reached an area of boggy marshland. You cannot cross it because you will sink down deep into the bog. But nearby is a herd of flying horses. You want to catch some so that you can ride them across the marshland. However, they are wild and very shy. If they see or hear you they will fly away immediately. Imagine how you and your friends can work together to capture and tame four of these flying horses ...

You have your horses now, so you can fly on them over the marshland. Hold on tight, hold the mane between your fingers. Feel the horses rise up into the air. Feel the wind rushing past your face. Look down into the land below you as you float high above it ...

Feel the gentle, rocking movement as the horse gallops through the air and hear the beatings of its magnificent wings.

Grip tight with your knees because when you reach the other side you come back down to Earth and slowly you slide off your horse, pat it gently and watch it soar away again ...

It is beginning to get dark and cold. You feel chilly as night begins to fall. You and your friends need to make or find shelter and somewhere to sleep. Imagine what you would do. Think of your preparations to make somewhere warm and comfortable for sleeping ...

Now you are tired and ready for sleep. You are cosy and relaxed and snug in your shelter. Feel the warmth and comfort as you drift off into a deep, calm sleep ...

Oh! it is morning now and time to continue on your journey. You have a deep forest to walk through. You look at it, it is wild and overgrown. The brambles and bushes are so thick, there is no way through. How are you going to make a way through? Picture in your mind what you and your friends could do to clear a path ...

Well done, because now, ahead is the land of High Ridge. You can see an endless line of mountains towering high in the sky. You only have to cross the mountain range to reach Mount Snowcap.

Think of yourself and your friends climbing ever higher. It is hard work. Picture the slow, gradual ascent – finding footholds, then somewhere to place your hands and hauling yourselves up. Higher you go, inch by inch by inch. Imagine how hard and tiring it is ...

Someone's foot slips and your friend slithers downwards into a gully. Somehow you and your friends have to rescue the person. How are you going to do this? ...

Congratulations! You have pulled them back up with you and at last you are nearing Mount Snowcap. You can see the cave entrance and the guarding dragon. What does it look like? Can you hear its loud roar and feel the heat of the flames as it bellows? ...

You must think of a plan to distract the dragon and lure it away from the entrance to the cave so that one of you can go in and capture the diamond.

What will you decide to do? How can you attract the dragon away so it leaves its position without it actually catching any of you? ...

But you've done it, the diamond is yours! Imagine how pleased and excited you feel and how relieved you are to have outwitted the dragon. Imagine how all of you are going to celebrate this wonderful success ...

A visit to a castle

Today we are going to have an imaginary tour around a castle.

Imagine that you are standing outside looking at the castle. What is it like? Does it have turrets and battlements? Is there a flag flying above it? ...

The castle has a moat around it. The water is deep and still and like a mirror and you can see the castle reflected in it. As you watch, the castle drawbridge is lowered. You walk across and hear your footsteps loudly on the wooden planks ...

Beyond the drawbridge is a courtyard. In the centre is a well. Picture yourself turning the handle to lower the bucket. Listen for the splash as it hits the water. Now you have to turn the handle the other way to raise the bucket. It is full of fresh, sparkling water and the handle is heavy and hard to turn ... You cannot resist tasting that fresh sparkling water.

You decide to go into the castle. There is a dark oak door with metal bars and studs on it. It is the biggest door you have ever seen and very heavy. You have to push your hardest to open it ...

Inside is a wide hall. On the walls are shields and spears, and around them are suits of armour. Think of these shiny metal suits and imagine what it would be like to wear one. Think of lifting your arms and trying to walk in a great heavy metal suit ...

As you walk through the castle, you can see big paintings of the people who have lived there. Imagine what they looked like in their old-fashioned clothes, imagine the look on their faces ...

You go now into the dining-room. It has a very long table that can seat forty people at least. It is wooden and very polished. On the table are forty plates, glasses and sets of silver cutlery, and there are beautiful glinting silver candelabra and silver salt and pepper pots. Everything is gleaming and shiny. Imagine all your class sitting around this table together ...

You come out of the dining-room and go down some steep stone steps. They are very old and worn and uneven. As you go down, it becomes colder and darker. You are underneath the castle, in the dungeons. It is damp and chilly and very gloomy because there are no windows down here.

Imagine the poor people who once got locked up in those dungeons, cramped into a small space ...

What would they have felt like ...?

You decide now to leave the damp darkness of the dungeons and reclimb the stairs.

You can see the light at the top of the stairs and you walk into a very large room which is the ball-room. Twinkling chandeliers hang from the ceiling. You look up at them and see the flashing glass lights. The ceiling is very beautiful. It has painted scenes and gold carvings. Imagine what it looks like. What can you see? What carvings can you imagine? ...

Think of the ball-room full of lords and ladies in their fine clothes and jewels.

Imagine an orchestra playing and the people dancing. The ladies' bright gowns are twirling and swishing and their fans are fluttering. Think of yourself there taking part in the dance. You know every step. You feel very confident and you are smiling ...

Now you leave the ball-room and climb the stone stairs to the very top of the castle. Out into the fresh air, you walk along the battlements. You look out over the countryside below you. It looks small and far away. What can you see from here? ...

Imagine the soldiers, many hundreds of years ago, walking along these battlements looking out for approaching enemies. Think of them wrapped in their cloaks, wearing helmets and carrying spears. What would they shout down to anyone they saw trying to creep along up to their castle.?

Imagine how you would look if you were King or Queen of this castle. Imagine how tall and strong and proud you feel. This all belongs to you and you resolve to be the kindest and most thoughtful King or Queen that has ever lived.

Case studies from two schools who are implementing the whole-school model

Newtown Primary School

Headteacher: Patrick Morgan

The context

Newtown Primary School is situated in a densely populated area of Gosport, near Portsmouth. There are currently 350 children on roll, 20% of whom are entitled to free school meals. A third are on the school's register of special educational needs.

When I arrived three years ago there were nine statemented children – four with emotional and behavioural difficulties. Many children were displaying challenging behaviour and although individual teachers were dealing very effectively with these children, there was no consistent behaviour policy in existence.

Getting it going

In my previous school I had introduced Jenny Mosley's Quality Circle Time system based on her book *Turn Your School Round* (Mosley 1993). This proved extremely successful and the Newtown staff were enthusiastic about developing something similar.

I felt it was important for my present staff to get a feel for the way that Jenny Mosley works. I arranged for her to demonstrate Circle Time for all the staff. Staff were so motivated by all the positive approaches and the openness with which the children spoke about their concerns that we agreed to adopt this as the basis of our behaviour policy. To train any new staff, I resolved, in the future, to timetable them to observe one or two experienced and trained members of staff. In this way we can sustain the model.

I then explained the elements of the policy to all groups of staff, emphasising that this would only work if all staff were committed to making it work. The aspects that were particularly appreciated were the following:

(a) Consistency – everybody was involved equally.
(b) Children were rewarded for behaving well (called Golden Time). Before introducing this policy, very often the only children to be rewarded were those that had behaved badly – causing resentment amongst both staff and children.
(c) Greater security in knowing how to deal with children who find it difficult to keep the rules (a visual warning first, then loss of Golden Time, which can be earned back by positive behaviour).
(d) A short but well-defined list of Golden Rules agreed by all the staff and children and expressed in positive terms.

People's responses

Having explained the system to school staff, I then held meetings for parents to inform them about the Golden Rules. (Subsequently, I discovered that a number of parents had adapted them for use at home – several children tell me they are written up in their bedrooms!)

Our dinner ladies particularly welcomed the new policy. They feel it has given them greater status and has helped other staff to appreciate what a difficult job they have to do. One of them, Michaela Robson, said, 'Usually all I need to do is to give a warning but if I need to take it further I know it will be taken seriously.'

From my point of view, it has eliminated the more inappropriate sanctions being used.

In the beginning some teachers were unsure how to maintain Circle Time within their class on a regular basis. Extra books have now been purchased and a greater emphasis is placed on listening to children and encouraging them to find their own solutions to problems. We have also timetabled Circle Time to happen at the same time in all classes. Many of our learning assistants attended a three-day listening skills course and Jenny was booked to help us review our policy, one year on.

Circle Time, along with Golden Time, is one of the highlights of the week for most of our children.

'We help each other.'
Luke (Year 4)

'In Circle Time we can talk about our problems and everybody listens.'
Sam (Year 5)

'I love Golden Time when we choose what we like to do.'
Matthew (Year 2)

'When I am upset I know there is someone I can talk to.'
Karl (Year 3)

Children 'beyond'

In a new development this year, I have begun a smaller 'therapeutic' group (nine children) for those children 'beyond' who find it difficult to keep the Golden Rules, often because they come from troubled home environments. I am working with one of the learning assistants and the support we are able to offer each other has been invaluable. The children in the group are engaged in creative work, as well as Circle Time, and this has gradually helped to raise their self-esteem. The results after nine months have been very positive – we are able to show that it works. Children who regularly missed Golden Time are now rarely in trouble.

Because we keep detailed records each week (who has lost Golden Time, how much, and what for) we are able to prove that the system works. We are able to target particular behaviours, such as rudeness, when these become a problem and we can also target those children who seem likely to have difficulties. I am able to report to governors on behaviour and this year we set a behaviour target for the school; for example, I am being gentle.

The main difficulty we face is constant review; there is a great need to keep the system fresh. We need to be sure that Golden Time is always exciting and that Circle Time is working properly. With the extra pressures on everybody's time it can be difficult to ensure that children are being listened to adequately, hence the need to train all the staff to listen to children. There are also problems of consistency, and both rewards and sanctions need to be reviewed regularly. It is, however, inevitable that children will know they are able to 'get away with it' more with some staff than others.

We need Circle Time, too

The other major difficulty, and one we have only partially solved, is the amount of support some staff need, particularly those who are dealing with the most troubled children. Not only do they need help to deal with the practical day-to-day situations that occur, but also with how to deal with the emotions which are often exposed. Staff have expressed guilt about the children we apparently have not been able to help. Perhaps we now need to explore the idea of bringing in a skilled facilitator to help run staff Circle Times.

Notwithstanding these problems, our behaviour policy is possibly one of the defining factors for Newtown School. When we were assessed recently for Investors in People, the assessor sub-titled his report 'Golden Rules – OK!'

NEWTOWN PRIMARY SCHOOL

INVESTORS IN PEOPLE ASSESSMENT
'GOLDEN RULES – OK!'

Clarity of purpose, focus on continual improvement and equal commitment to all people are strong evidence at Newtown that you can touch it!

There are many examples of Newtown demonstrating that it has invested a great deal of time and effort in making the school a successful organisation. One such example gives rise to the sub-title of this report: Golden Rules – OK!

Patrick Morgan, Headteacher, heard about 'Golden Time', a technique for improving behaviour in school children. He bought the book and invited the author to speak to all staff during one of their Inset training days. At this meeting the purpose of Golden Time was discussed and all staff were invited to help to develop Newtown's policy towards improving behaviour.

Simply, Golden Time involves enjoying a weekly quality playtime within class-time. Equally, penalty points (loss of time) can be awarded and this is referred to as 'Blue Stickers'! After some resistance, due to 'time pressures', 'new approach to old problems' etc., a policy was developed and embraced by all. Within the policy, Golden Rules were formulated and these were distributed throughout Newtown.

Everyone spoken to relates to Golden Time and Golden Rules as a major contribution to Newtown meeting its declared aims and objectives. 'I've even seen Golden Rules in a parent's kitchen,' remarked one teacher. 'I had to warn a teacher with a blue sticker the other day,' said a Supervisory Assistant.

Golden Rules encapsulate Newtown's approach to developing an organisation whereby all staff understand what the organisation is trying to achieve.

Stephen Gould – Assessor
February 1998

EXTRACTS FROM OFSTED REPORT RELATING TO THE WHOLE-SCHOOL QUALITY CIRCLE TIME MODEL

NEWTOWN PRIMARY SCHOOL

The values the school promotes are reflected in the attention that is paid to the pupils' spiritual, moral, social and cultural development. It is also seen in the growing strength of relationships, in the teamwork and the co-operation shown at every level and in the success of the school's behaviour management strategies. The quality of pastoral care is high and health and safety matters are given a high priority.

The pupils co-operate well together in pairs or small groups and from an early age are able to work unsupervised. Parents express satisfaction with pupils' behaviour and approve of the emphasis placed on rewarding good behaviour.

There are good relationships between pupils and all the adults working in the school. There is no evidence of inappropriate behaviour, such as bullying or racial harassment towards any particular individuals or groups of pupils. When the pupils have opportunities, such as circle time, to listen to each other they do so attentively, respecting each other's views.

Personal and social education is taught very effectively through other subjects and through circle time.

There is particular emphasis on Christian principles and the Golden Rules that aim to develop good personal and moral behaviour. Throughout the school a high priority is given to the pupils' spiritual, moral, social and cultural development. Pupils respond positively and in their relationships they strive to be polite and helpful to each other and to all the adults with whom they come into contact. Pupils are taught, and understand, the difference between right and wrong. During the day the teachers and all other adults emphasise the importance of kindness, honesty and respect for others' property.

That the school is largely successful in achieving its aims is seen in the secure and caring learning environment that has been created and in the positive working atmosphere, and good relationships that are characteristic of the classrooms throughout the school.

The behaviour policy is proving to be particularly successful; it rewards good behaviour whilst providing sanctions for poor behaviour, but allowing the latter to be redeemed. Careful monitoring has allowed the school to focus on specific pupils with poor behaviour, and there are indications of significant improvements; particularly for some boys.

Classroom relationships are good, the pupils work responsibly and harmoniously together in both small and large groups. This is a strength of the school.

Jack Lobley School

Deputy head:
Alice Witherow

School context

Jack Lobley Primary School serves an area of high social deprivation in Tilbury, Essex. Essex County Council have recognised this; the school receives the highest social factor funding of any school in the county. Children with special needs make up 50% of the school population, which has a turnover rate of 10%. The school was opened in 1972 and has since then had five headteachers. The current headteacher has been in post for five years and has appointed all but two of the thirty staff (teachers and support staff) himself. The high turnover of staff and the problems inherent in a school population with such demanding needs make it a challenging school to work in.

The main school is open with four additional relocatable classrooms. A nursery unit which takes children at 3, for one year, feeds into the Early Years Unit, with another nine classes making up Key Stages 1 and 2. The school roll including the nursery rests at around 350 pupils.

Staffing ratios are high, with each class benefiting from a full-time teaching assistant. A central management team consists of the head and deputy along with other post holders. All meetings are open to all staff, with two regular staff meetings weekly plus a management meeting on a Wednesday.

This case study spans from 1992 until the present day and aims to examine the influence of the Quality Circle Time model in enhancing the behaviour and therefore the achievement of pupils within the school.

The school in 1992/93

In 1993, Tilbury was named by HMI1 as an area failing to give children a quality education. Within the town the four primary schools and one secondary joined together to form an initiative to raise standards. This had huge financial implications for the school and brought assistance in the form of additional funding and support.

In the third term of 1993 Jack Lobley School appointed a new headteacher. His first task was to improve behaviour at the school. At the time children were regularly off task, many exhibited violent and aggressive behaviour to both children and staff and on several occasions children had to be removed by the police – so extreme was their behaviour that they could not be contained within the school.

Staff were difficult to recruit and the current staff, five of whom had already handed in resignations, were demoralised. Many of these teachers had themselves been abused by children and, despite the best efforts of staff, there was no sense of support for each other, or purpose or vision, in working with these children.

For a newly appointed head in his first headship the responsibility was immense. Coupled with appointing new staff – most of whom were NQTs – he had to face a barrage of criticism from the local community when the press labelled Tilbury 'Town of Dunces'.

Raising staff morale

Jenny Mosley's Quality Circle Time model focuses a great deal of attention on the needs of staff. Implicit to the model is the need for schools to address behaviour management issues through supporting staff; by sharing their visions for the school, sharing their needs from a behaviour management system, supporting each other in an ethos which allows a democratic voice for all and engendering a sense of equal responsibility for all children amongst all staff.

At Jack Lobley one of the first issues that needed to be addressed was the lack of shared responsibility. Classes were organised purely according to numbers and some classes consequently had several children with extreme behavioural problems while other classes had relatively few. Teachers took responsibility for their own children and there was little mixing between Key Stages 1 and 2.

In appointing a member of staff to the unusual post of behaviour coordinator, the headteacher went some way in building on the strength of individual staff. The new behaviour coordinator was in her second year of teaching and had gained some credibility as an NQT in being able to work with demanding children. As a team the head and the behaviour coordinator agreed to hold monthly support meetings for staff to allow them to express their concerns about individual children, and to focus on the needs of the school in developing a whole-school strategy.

At this stage the school was still operating a crisis management strategy, responding to the needs of children as situations arose. By implementing monthly meetings about behaviour management, staff were given the opportunity to express their concerns free of criticism and to feel listened to and valued. It was also accepted at these meetings that responsibility for children rested not with the individual teacher, nor with the headteacher, but with all staff equally; and that by supporting each other through discussion, sharing and listening a real impact could be made. Different strategies were discussed and agreement was reached over using rules and rewards. Attention was turned to using Circle Time as a strategy with children as the behaviour coordinator had found it to be successful in her first year.

The circle meetings for staff were in many ways the turning point for the children. Through collective responsibility an ethos was created in which children felt secure and where discipline was far more consistent. Teachers did not feel they were on their own if their classes contained particularly difficult children and responsibility did not rest solely with the headteacher, who previously was expected to intervene at the stage when it became obvious that the child was 'beyond'.

To this day the single factor that is most noticeable about the school is the level of support that colleagues have for each other and the opportunities for teachers to discuss the different strategies they employ with difficult children.

In the academic year 1993/94 weekly Circle Time meetings with children were still limited to individual class teachers who felt confident in the model. Whole-school issues such as staff support and mental health plans had been addressed largely by the monthly meetings, and where Circle Time was used effectively levels of cooperation and improvements in class behaviour were noticeable. The incidence of injury, police support and senior staff intervention had lessened and the school was ready to progress to the next stage.

OFSTED

At the start of 1994/95 the school was notified that it was to be inspected by OFSTED. The behaviour of children was still a major concern and it was felt very strongly by staff that everyone should be involved in circle work with their classes. The behaviour coordinator, who had attended a one-day course on Circle Time with Jenny Mosley, began to share ideas and teach other staff. The response from the children was overwhelming. They enjoyed the opportunity to share, they liked the sense of being listened to, and the cooperation and sense of identity within the school dramatically improved. Furthermore, OFSTED were keen to recognise this as a major strength of the school.

To quote the OFSTED report (HMI 1995), Circle Time is a well-structured activity, which enables:

> **pupils to reflect on personal experiences, to listen to the opinions of others and to express their own views. Sensitivity on the part of the teachers means that these sessions make a significant contribution to the pupils' personal and social development.**

Developing the model further

In the summer of 1996, the school's behaviour coordinator attended a week's residential training course with Jenny Mosley and became an accredited Quality Circle Time trainer. On her return to school, it was agreed that all staff would readily benefit from full training in the model and that areas previously underdeveloped in the model could be extended. Again, there had been a high turnover of staff and therefore a commitment from senior management to developing the model and empowering staff was crucial.

A six-week twilight course was run and staff examined issues of self-esteem, the importance of listening systems and the importance of conflict resolution as part of the model. Some staff also agreed to try Golden Time with children as part of the school's reward system. In the upper school, where this was most developed, children responded very positively. One to one (Bubble I–I time) and Think Books, both part of the Quality Circle Time model, also gave children the security of knowing that they would always be listened to. Parents were keen to understand what was going on and spoke enthusiastically about how secure their children felt and how confident they were that issues could be dealt with.

Aspects of the weekly circle meeting began to transfer into other areas of working. When discussing one day the need to be sensitive when helping a writing partner edit their work, a year-5 child suggested to his teacher, 'Why don't we use: Would it help if you/Would it help if I?'; one of the key scripts of the Open Forum!

Lunchtimes

Lunchtimes are always difficult in schools, and this was certainly true for Jack Lobley. This is the next area of development for the school. Aspects of the Quality Circle Time model are being used. Areas of the playground are organised for specific activities and lunchtime staff really do play with the children. Teachers, too, help teach playground games and equipment is available for children to play with.

There is an opportunity for children to come off the playground and work with an assistant inside, playing games and making things. An allotment is available; children may join the allotment society and help grow things. Some children are referred to these alternative activities and others choose to join. The system is fairly successful, with fewer teachers having to leave the staffroom to attend to behaviour incidents.

Conclusion

This year the school hosted a Quality Circle Time day to which other schools came to see what had been done and find out why the school believed in Quality Circle Time. It is a different institution from the one that was in existence six years ago. Circle Time has had a key influence on this. Responding to an evaluation of the day, one delegate reported as follows after having seen Circle Time:

> **I hope that at my daughter's new school she is
> treated with the same respect that I have seen today.
> This school has got it right when dealing with the
> mental health of children.**

There is still work to be done in developing all the aspects of the Quality Circle Time model. As ever, new staff need to be trained when they come to the school; it is daunting to find that even those who have previous experience of Circle Time may have been misinformed or are misusing aspects of the model.

If a school facing the challenges that face Jack Lobley can find this model so beneficial, then the model has a role to play in the future of behaviour management in schools throughout the UK.

References: see Appendix 2.

APPENDIX
2

Resources

ACCREDITED, SPECIALIST TRAINERS ONLY!

Our research and experience, has revealed that the reason this model becomes diluted and vulnerable, is because there are trainers, either from LEAs or from other sources, such as charities, who give courses based on my work, yet they themselves have either only attended a one day course – or are working using my books. I run indepth courses and then issue the accompanying certificates. Please check the training of your consultant in this model, and if they haven't been trained by myself, you are either getting a watered down version or it is not our model.

There are many different Circle Time approaches around – but ours is a quality whole-school model that incorporates very firm structures and recommendations for every part of a school day.

Training –
Jenny Mosley
Inset courses

The following courses are available from a team of highly qualified and experienced consultants who can be contacted through:

Jenny Mosley Consultancies
8 Westbourne Road
Trowbridge
Wiltshire
BA14 0AJ
 Tel: 01225 767157
Fax: 01225 755631

- **Promoting Happier Lunchtimes**
- **Turn Your School Round – an introduction**
- **A Whole-School Approach to building self-esteem through Circle Time**

→ **Assessing the effectiveness of your self-esteem, anti-bullying and positive behaviour policies**

⇢ **Raising morale through team-building**

→ **Practical activities to maintain and develop the power of Circle Time**

⇢ **Equal opportunities**

→ **Curriculum enrichment**

⇢ **Drama and creative arts**

→ **Play therapy: an introduction course**

⇢ **Writing effective IEPs through Circle Time**

Training the Trainer courses

Key people may be trained either to go back to their school or their LEA as certified trainers responsible for supporting all adults and children in their community through the Jenny Mosley model. Currently Jenny Mosley Consultancies are hosting a series of on-going five-day courses led by Jenny. For further information contact Kay Hardwick, 37 Victoria Road, Trowbridge, Wiltshire BA14 7LH. Tel: 01225 350797. Fax: 01225 753613. email:jm.conferences@cableinet.co.uk

Training support for your workplace

Jenny Mosley Consultancies have well-trained personnel, experienced in all aspects of the Quality Circle Time model, who are available to visit your workplace to give courses and workshops to all your teaching and support staff.

They run both 'closure' and 'in-school' days.

○ In a closure day, all staff – teachers, lunchtime supervisors, ancillary and administration staff – are invited to participate, with the focus on aspects of the Circle Time model including team-building and developing moral values through Golden Rules, incentives and sanctions and ideas for happier lunchtimes.

○ During the in-school day, the school does not close, and the Circle Time method is demonstrated with whole classes of children observed by a range of staff. In addition to this, Circle Time meetings are held for lunchtime supervisors and an action plan for the school is considered with key members of staff.

Jenny Mosley
training manuals and resources

Mosley, J. (1993) *Turn Your School Round*, LDA.

This book clearly outlines the Quality Circle Time model to enable a whole school to initiate its own policy on self-esteem and positive behaviour. The book contains the rationale behind the approach, the steps you need to take to develop a whole-school policy and Circle Time sessions to use with teachers, pupils, support staff, governors and parents.

" Jenny Mosley's book presents a **very persuasive** rationale for adopting Circle Time as an integral part of the school's curriculum. *Turn Your School Round* is an ambitious book ... The methods proposed by Jenny Mosley are *informed* by the recognition that self-esteem is central to promoting appropriate behaviour in adults and children ... I feel that this book is an *invaluable resource* for schools and can be **recommended** to anyone who works with children. "

Rory Gordon,
Special Children

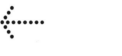

" I'm *recommending* *Turn Your School Round* as **a must for every school**. There are so may good ideas and it's such *a delight* to read. "

Primary Headteacher

" The book is *great*, **useful**, full of helpful *practical* ideas, thought provoking, creative, easy to follow, well presented, *teacher friendly*, but above all, (for me) of real benefit to schools and children ... it's all about central issues for schools. "

Senior Educational Psychologist

Mosley, J. (1996) *Quality Circle Time*, LDA

The essential handbook for using Circle Time in the primary classroom. As well as containing the theoretical underpinnings of Circle Time, this book has over 200 activities for Circle Time sessions, problems encountered by Circle Time users with suggested solutions and information on training and support.

" This is an extremely practical book with a sound theoretical underpinning which would be well placed in the hands of every primary teacher in the UK."
Special Children

" I instantly **warmed** to Ms Mosley's amiable writing style and found myself **trusting** her as she displayed an obvious and ***thorough understanding*** of ground floor teaching reality."
Emotional and Behavioural Difficulties Journal

" Here was someone who put the *teacher first* and acknowledged that they had to **find time for themselves** and their families and suggested how that time could be found. At last teachers are being treated like ***human beings*** instead of political footballs."
Primary School Manager

Self-Esteem Builders

Mosley, J. (1996) *Golden Rules Posters*, LDA

Eye-catching posters to encourage pupils to keep the Golden Rules both in and out of the school building.

Seven A4 class Golden Rules and one A2 PVC playground rules.

Mosley, J. (1996) *Class Target Sheets*, LDA

Two A2 posters, one space and one underwater scene. The reusable stars and fish are placed on the posters by children who have reached their class targets, and so work together to complete the picture.

Mosley, J. (1996) *Reward Certificates*, LDA

Certificates to reward pupils for a whole range of behaviours, attitudes and achievements; e.g. Congratulations for deciding to improve, Congratulations for keeping all the Golden Rules at lunchtime, Congratulations for reaching your chosen target. Seventy-two A5 certificates (12 x 6 designs).

" No one who has seen this kind of work done properly can be in any doubt that these techniques are *extremely useful* and can **revolutionise** both children's behaviour and the underlying *feelings and attitudes* that shape it. "

Review of Self-esteem Builders,
TES Resources

Mosley, J. (1996) *Responsibility Badges*, LDA

Nine reusable badges for selected children to wear; e.g. I am trying to be calm today, I'm special child of the week, I am a playground helper.

Mosley, J. (1996) *Stickers*, LDA

Purposeful and specific stickers divided into three categories to mirror the Quality Circle Time model:

Golden Rules (e.g. Well done for being kind)
Lunchtimes (e.g. We like the way you queue calmly)
Circle Time (e.g. I like noticing the good in people).
360 stickers in 36 designs.

Mosley, J. (1999) *Quality Circle Time Kit*, LDA

A bag full of high quality resources; 2 puppets, 2 speaking objects, a rainstick, a blindfold, a cassette tape, a treasure chest and a reversible cloak. The kit contains Circle Time ideas using the kit contents.

Mosley, J. (2000) *Quality Circle Time Video*, LDA

In this 30 minute video, Jenny Mosley demonstrates how to structure a class circle time. The video outlines the basic structure of a circle time session with both reception and year 6 classes.

" This is a well put together kit which can be used in a variety of ways. "
Nursery Equipment

Mosley, J. (1992) *Create Happier Lunchtimes,*
Wiltshire Education Advisory Services,
County Hall, Trowbridge, Wiltshire

Contains advice on how midday supervisors can achieve respectful relationships with the children and other adults in this community. Useful tips on lunchtime organisation. Great ideas for wet playtimes.

Mosley, J. (1996) *Photocopiable Materials for Use with the Jenny Mosley Circle Time Model,* **Positive Press**

Photocopiable materials to support the Quality Circle Time model. Items include; a thank-you letter, warning cards, reminder notes and an invitation to Circle Time.

Report on the Use of Circle Time in Wiltshire Primary Schools (1998)

Sponsored by The Body Shop Foundation, it is an indepth qualitative study of Circle Time in Wiltshire School undertaken by CL10 at Bristol University. Available from Jenny Mosley Consultancies.

Goldthorpe, M. (1998) *Effective IEPs through Circle Time,* **LDA**

A practical book written by one of Jenny's accredited consultants, demonstrating how to write genuinely effective Individual Education Plans for pupils with emotional and behavioural difficulties through class Circle Times.

" Margaret's book *describes in detail* how to use circle time in the construction of *individual education plans* for pupils with emotional and behavioural difficulties. "

Gerald Haigh,
TES Primary.

Goldthorpe, M. (1998) *Poems for Circle Time and Literacy Hour*, LDA

A charming, photocopiable collection of illustrated poems, which can be used in the whole-class component of the Literacy Hour. Guidelines are also given about how to incorporate the poems into Circle Time sessions later, in order to discuss pupils' personal response to the issues raised.

Topics covered include: saying goodbye to a parent, friendships, sharing, concentrating, bullying, feeling ill, feeling left out, school dinners and school trips.

References

Bandura, A. (1977) *Social Learning Theory*. London, Prentice Hall Inc.

Burns, R. (1982) *Self Concept Development and Education*. Holt, Rinehart and Winston.

Cooley, C. H. (1964) *Human Nature and the Social Order*. New York, Schocken.

Gardner, H. (1993) *Multiple Intelligence – The Theory in Practice*. London, Basic Books.

Goldthorpe, M. (1998) *Effective IEPs through Circle Time*. Cambridge, LDA.

Goldthorpe, M. (1998) *Poems for Circle Time and Literacy Hour*. Cambridge, LDA.

Goleman, D. (1996) *Emotional Intelligence*. London, Bloomsbury.

HMI (1995) *Access and Achievement in Urban Education*.

Hopkins, Dr. D. (1991) *Improving the Quality of Education for All*. Cambridge, University of Cambridge, Institute of Education.

Klein, M. (1929) *Personification in the play of children*. J. Pscho-An; 10:193-204.

Maslow, A. H. *Motivation and Personality*. (3rd edition). New York, Harper and Row.

Maslow, A. H. *Towards a Psychology of Being*. New York, Van Nostrand Reinholt.

Mead, G. H. (1934) *Mind, Self and Society*. Chicago, University of Chicago Press.

Moreno, J. H. (1934) *Who Shall Survive?* New York, Beacon House.

Mosley, J. (1989) *All Round Success*. Trowbridge, Wiltshire Education Authority.

Mosley, J. (1993) *Turn Your School Round*. Cambridge, LDA.

Mosley, J. (1996) *Quality Circle Time*. Cambridge, LDA.

Mosley, J. and E. Gillibrand (1995) *She Who Dares Wins*. London, HarperCollins.

Mosley, J. and E. Gillibrand (1997) *When I Go to Work I Feel Guilty*. London, HarperCollins.

Perls (1969) *Gestalt Therapy Verbatum*. Lafayette, Real People Press.

QCA (1998) *Initial Report on Education for Citizenship and the Teaching of Democracy in Schools*. London, QCA.

Rogers, C. (1961) *On Becoming a Person*. Boston, Houghton Mifflin.

Rotter, J. B., (1996) *Generalised expectations for internal versus external control of reinforcement*. Psychological Monogram 80, No. 609.

Other titles of interest

Ayres, H., Clarke. D. & Murray A. (1995) *Perspectives on Behaviour – a practical guide to effective interventions for teachers*. London, David Fulton.

Dryden, G. & Dr. Vos, J. (1994) *The Learning Revolution*. Bucks, Accelerated Learning Systems Ltd.

Erricker, C. & J., Editors (2000) *A Calmer Classroom, Clearer Minds: Introducing Meditation into Education*. Cassell.

Glasser, W. (MD). (1965) *Reality Therapy – a new approach to psychiatry*. London, Harper & Row Publishers.

Farrington, L. & Highfield Junior School, Plymouth. (1997) *Changing Our School – promoting positive behaviour*. Sponsored by the Calouste Gulbenkian Foundation. Published by Highfield Junior School & The Institute of Education, University of London.

Hannaford, C. Ph. D. (1995) *Smart Moves – why learning is not all in your head*. Virginia, USA, Great Ocean Publishers, Arlington.

O'Donohue. (1997) *Anam Cara – spiritual wisdom from the celtic world*. London, Transworld Publishers.

Rogers, C. (1983) *Freedom to Learn – for the 80's*. London, Charles E, Merrill Publishing Company.